Ethical Issues in Family Therapy

edited by

Sue Walrond-Skinner
and David Watson

ROUTLEDGE & KEGAN PAUL

London and New York

First published in 1987 by
Routledge & Kegan Paul Ltd
11 New Fetter Lane, London EC4P 4EE

Published in the USA by
Routledge & Kegan Paul Inc.
in association with Methuen Inc.
29 West 35th Street, New York, NY 10001

Set in 10/12 Bembo
by Witwell Ltd, Liverpool
and printed in Great Britain
by Billings, Worcester.

Library of Congress Cataloging in Publication Data
Ethical issues in family therapy.

Bibliography: p.
Includes index.
1. Family psychotherapy—Moral and ethical
aspects. I. Walrond-Skinner, Sue. II. Watson,
David, 1946– . [DNLM: 1. Ethics.
2. Family Therapy. WM 430.5.F2 E837]
RC488.5.E85 1987 174'.2 87–4562

British Library CIP Data also available
ISBN 0–7102–1196–1 (c)
0–7102–1092–2 (p)

CONTENTS

NOTES ON CONTRIBUTORS

John Carpenter graduated in psychology and qualified in social work. He has worked with single homeless people, young offenders, in hospitals and a child guidance clinic. At present he holds a joint appointment to the Departments of Social Work and Mental Health at Bristol University and to Avon Social Services Department. He practises family therapy at a psychiatric day hospital in Weston-super-Mare. He is co-editor (with Andy Treacher) of *Using Family Therapy*.

Andrew Collier was born in London in 1944, and studied at London University. He has taught philosophy at Warwick and Sussex Universities, and (currently) at University College of North Wales, Bangor. He is the author of a book on R. D. Laing, and three essays in the series *Issues in Marxist Philosophy*, edited by John Mepham and David Ruben. He has also contributed to the journals *Radical Philosophy* and *International Socialism* on philosophical questions raised by the work of Marx and Freud. He is currently writing a book on realism in the philosophy of social science.

Douglas Haldane was an NHS consultant in child and family psychiatry and later a Senior Lecturer in a university department of mental health, with particular responsibilities for teaching and training in psychotherapy. He has been Vice-Chairman of the Association for Family Therapy, Editor of its Newsletter and Convenor of its Sub-Committee on Ethics. He is now in private practice as a psychotherapist and as a freelance consultant.

Philip Kingston is a Lecturer in Social Work at Bristol University and an associate of the Family Institute at Cardiff. He is married with three grown-up children. His interests include the relationship between the therapist's own family and his/her professional work with families; the relevance of a sociological perspective to work with families; and the development of methods of supervision and consultation.

Richard Lindley is the author of *Autonomy*, 1986, and is interested in the relationship between what people want and their long term interests: autonomy versus welfare? He co-authored an introduction to philosophy called *What Philosophy Does*, 1978, in which he discussed the problem of the compulsory treatment of mental disorders. He has been a lecturer in philosophy at Bradford University in the School of Human Studies, since 1975, and is a member of the MOSAIC interdisciplinary research colloquium on morality, and a member of the executive committee of the Society for Applied Philosophy.

Una McCluskey graduated in social science and qualified as a social worker. She trained in analytical group work at the Scottish Institute of Human Relations, worked for five years in a Department of Child and Family Psychiatry in Fife, and was active in the development of new in-patient facilities for whole families. In 1977 she joined the executive of the Association of Family Therapy for four years. She was a member of the training sub-committee and convenor of the sub-committee on accreditation for family therapists. She worked at Barnardo's in Edinburgh as a senior family case-worker before joining the staff of the social work course at York University. She is actively engaged in training family therapists in the psychiatric services in York, and continues to work with clients, groups and organisations.

Adam Morton teaches in the Philosophy department at the University of Bristol, and has two main research interests. One is the formal analysis of language and the other is the borderline between the philosophy of mind and ethics. He is now writing a book about moral and practical dilemmas.

Andy Treacher was Lecturer in Mental Health, Department of Mental Health, University of Bristol, where he taught psychology to medical students and clinical psychology to psychology students. Between 1976 and 1978 he trained (part-time) as a clinical psychologist, and also spent a sabbatical six months at the Family Institute, Cardiff, training as a family therapist with Brian Cade and Sue Walrond-Skinner. Currently he is employed in an Honorary capacity as a Clinical Psychologist at Barrow Hospital, but he also undertakes peripatetic consultancy work including a session at Chippenham Child Guidance Clinic. For the last 5 years he has been an active member of the Training Sub-Committee of the Association for Family Therapy. He has co-authored *Psychiatry Observed*, 1978, and co-edited a handbook of family therapy, *Using Family Therapy*, 1984.

Sue Walrond-Skinner trained as a social worker and later as a family therapist. She has been in practice as a family therapist for the past 16 years. From 1971 to 1977 she helped to start the Family Institute in Cardiff, specialising in practice, teaching and research into family therapy. She has continued teaching family therapy alongside practising it, since moving to Bristol in 1977. She is a founder member of the Association for Family Therapy. Publications include *Family Therapy – the treatment of natural systems*, 1976, *Dictionary of Psychotherapy*, 1986 and as editor, *Family and Marital Psychotherapy*, 1979 and *Developments in Family Therapy*.

David Watson is lecturer in Social Administration at the University of Bristol. His publications in the field of philosophy and social policy include *Caring for Strangers*, 1980, and, as editor, *A Code of Ethics for Social Work – the second step*, 1985.

PREFACE

The collection of essays published in this volume may be seen as fruit of the capacity for growth in the usually unassociated backgrounds of their authors. Family therapists have become more conscious of the moral issues raised by their forms of intervention and have been willing to draw upon sources outside their membership and conventional training. Access to the literature and methods of moral philosophy has come in a number of ways, including workshops conducted by David Watson and therapists John Carpenter, Arnon Bentovim and Hugh Jenkins, at the Annual Conferences of 1982 and 1983. In recent years moral and political philosophers have returned to consideration of substantive issues and again come to see their methods as part of a collaborative effort with others possessing other essential skills and experience, though *precisely* what each might offer and learn, as is the way with growth, is always to be *discovered*.

Located at the University of Bristol, we were well-placed to develop the proposal which attracted the support of the Sir Halley Stewart Trust and, in the pleasant setting of Burwalls, to draw together on three occasions a small-enough group of family therapists and philosophers known to us as sympathetic to such collaboration. The resulting essays record only a fraction of our agenda and less still of the possible agenda, but we have at least got beyond the conventional chapter of instruction and re-assurance, under the heading 'Ethical Issues', which has to date concluded so many books on family therapy.

Sue Walrond-Skinner
David Watson

ACKNOWLEDGMENTS

All those whose work is published here were members of a series of workshops kindly supported by the Sir Halley Stewart Trust. Funding is rarely available for thinking or discussion, and we must thank the Trustees for recognising that the relief of suffering may be advanced by these means. Keith Graham, Tony Gale and Brian Cade were also members of the workshops, and we should like to acknowledge their help. Errollyn Bruce and Gwynn Davis offered additional comment to particular authors; Belinda Maggs typed the manuscript. We should also like to thank the Editor for permission to include, in chapter 9, part of the article by Philip Kingston which appeared in the *Journal of Family Therapy* (4, 1982, pp.211–27).

INTRODUCTION

Sue Walrond-Skinner

The task of this book is to outline some of the ethical issues which confront the family therapist in the course of his or her work; to make explicit some of the assumptions which inform that work, and to link them to existing more general discussions of ethical issues within the field of psychotherapy as a whole.

Psychotherapy raises ethical issues which have become more complex with the increased diversity of method and wider ranges of technical equipment now at our disposal. Various codes of practice have been established by professional associations and institutes which offer guidance for the practitioner and some protection for the patient or family; but in Britain, despite the recommendations of the Foster Report in 1971, the practice of psychotherapists remains un-controlled by law. Legal regulation does not ensure ethical practice, but it may identify those activities which are properly subject to legal review and legal remedy, so that at least one conception of ethical practice is sanctioned. (Watson, 1985, illustrates this approach as it pertains to the practice of social work.)

If we take a very broad perspective to begin with we may note that the practice of psychotherapy, as such, has been criticised as being unethical by writers such as Foucault, Szasz, Illich and others because, as they see it, psychotherapy has an inherent tendency to represent dominant cultural beliefs and thus to act as a normalising and therefore as a repressive agent of society. These writers are particularly critical of the way in which the individual is measured against what they would regard as artificial, societal norms of mental health in the diagnosis of pathology, often using assumptions derived from the medical model which they see as being inappropriate to emotional, psychological and situational difficulties. These views are well summarised by Kennedy (1981) and are explored from a different point of view by writers such as Downie (1971) in their discussions of the relative merits of punishment or treatment for crimes committed.

1

Ethical issues arise from various aspects of the therapeutic process: from deficiencies in the personality, skill and competence of the therapist; from the nature of the therapeutic relationship; from the method and techniques of therapy being employed; from the type of patient/family being treated; and from the demands made by third parties upon the therapeutic process.

First, the therapist variable. The contributions to the therapeutic process made by the therapist include his or her personality make-up, his or her own varying emotional needs, knowledge, technical skill and therapeutic experience, all of which contribute to his or her competence, or lack of it, as a therapist. All forms of psychotherapy recognise the therapist variable as an important ingredient in the therapeutic process, although to varying degrees, and in family therapy, likewise, the therapist's personality, style, experience and technical skill are viewed as major factors in bringing about a positive outcome. However, although the personality of the therapist has been found to be critical in some studies of patient deterioration in individual psychotherapy, no attempt has been made to assess the psychonoxious effects of therapist personality in family therapy, or to link this factor with negative outcomes. Moreover, in most forms of individual therapy, the provision of rigorous and often quite prolonged training protects the patient to some extent from the effects of gross deficits in the therapist's personality, knowledge and skill, and, by requiring established lengths of supervised practice prior to accreditation, minimal levels of experience are safeguarded. In family therapy, as we know, there are as yet few provisions for, or recognition of, formal training of a general and basic nature and of reasonable duration. Such training as exists rarely provides an adequate grounding in the ethical considerations of family treatment, though Piercey *et al.* (1983) describe a notable exception.

Second, the relationship itself between therapist and family, involving the meshing together of the needs, strengths and weaknesses of the two parties, poses many areas of potential difficulty. Beyond the possibility of blatant, conscious dishonesty or immoral behaviour, the therapist's counter-transference may lead him or her to exploit the family, or individuals within it, on an unconscious level. The need to be helpful, avoid hostility, be nurturant, controlling, potent, act as a rescuer or simply 'be successful' may all lead the therapist to collude with pressure from the family or third parties or to act out his or her sexual attraction or punitive impulses towards one or more family members. Sex therapy creates particular ethical dilemmas in this respect and there appears to be increasing evidence of therapists acting out their sexual attraction to their patients (Dahlberg, 1970; Kardener *et al.*, 1973; Store, 1976).

General value conflicts of many different kinds may get subsumed within rather than confronted by, the therapist's assumptions about the families' or identified patients' problems. Hines and Hare-Mustin (1981) point out how 'therapists are often unaware of the extent to which their own personal and professional values govern therapeutic moves, to the exclusion of recognising the uniqueness of the family situation and the net effect of disturbing the family system' (p. 436). Tsoi-Hoshmund (1976) has drawn attention to the way in which changing social values (e.g. arising out of the development of feminism) need to be taken account of in practice. Few feminists would be happy about either Skynner's (1976) or Minuchin's (1974) description of the normal, healthy executive subsystem as that which includes a dominant male. Moreover, the necessary therapeutic effort to win what Whitaker (1975) describes as the 'battle for initiative and control' of the therapy may nevertheless create a power imbalance in the therapists' favour, especially when working with a team, and this may lead to the use of techniques designed to address psychological problems, to attack instead the family's different and threatening value system.

Third, there may be more complex issues to be faced in the potential conflict between individual and group than are usually acknowledged or acted upon in family therapy. If we affirm relationships as entities in themselves, 'more than' and over and above the individuals which comprise them, we may lose an essential perspective on the individual in his or her own right. For example, what principles guide us when the needs and rights of individual family members are in profound conflict? Dell (1980) suggests that constructs such as power and personal responsibility are epistemologically flawed; for him, the concept of individual responsibility is 'an epistemological error'. But is the basic systemic premise of levelling the culpability of all family members down to the same point, so that individual actions are interchangeable and which family member presents the symptom or problem is viewed as 'arbitrary', ethically justifiable, however sound it may appear to be technically? Often such a levelling, using techniques such as the positive connotation, flies in the face of common conceptions of justice, particularly when we are faced with gross disparity in the power relationship of the conflicting parties. Trying to unlock the family's self-defeating 'blame-game' in these ways may produce ethical dilemmas which we have not yet fully faced.

Fourth, is it actually the case that 'nothing is good or bad but thinking makes it so'? Is all content actually reduceable to process in this way? Clearly one of the major leaps forward in the family therapy field is the recognition and understanding of process, but is content therefore completely irrelevant? Bandler and Grinder (1976) remark that 'when people come to us in therapy expressing pain and dissatisfaction, the limitations that they experience are typically in their *representation* of the world, not in the world itself' (p. 179). Undoubtedly this is a powerful therapeutic position which we all rightly adopt with many families, but an approach which is *typically* appropriate is not necessarily *always* appropriate. Does what Watzlawick calls the 'gentle art of refraining' involve us living permanently in a looking-glass world of backwards-way-round realities? I suspect that this is where family therapists most need our philosopher colleagues to help us talk more clearly and rationally about truth, reality and personal autonomy.

Fifth, we have to face the familiar consequentialist means/ends tension when weighing the use of many of our most effective techniques. Consequentialists, as Singer (1980) points out, 'start not with moral rules but with goals. They assess actions by the extent to which they further these goals' (p. 3). Family therapy draws on a whole range of techniques used in other methods of psychotherapy, so some of these problems of the legitimation of the means by the effective achievement of the ends have been addressed elsewhere. Directive therapies such as behaviour therapy, behaviour modification, strategic therapy, provocative therapy, rational-emotive therapy, etc. are specific and proactive in their techniques and they are therefore more obviously open to scrutiny for potential abuse. Non-directive approaches employ more reactive techniques, but the fact that social influence has been shown to operate subtly in all therapeutic relationships means that psychoanalytic and humanistic approaches to family therapy can also be problematic. Premature in-depth interpretations or pressure to self-disclose, for example, may be as intrusive and perhaps unacceptable (even if effective) as more obviously intrusive, directive techniques. The exercise of covert control in strategic therapy and the use of non-compliance based techniques such as symptom prescription, paradoxical injunctions and the therapeutic double bind raises questions about the ethics of reducing or eliminating the full participation and consent of the family in its treatment and its right to self-determination, *if* such a right can be deemed to exist for a family as distinct from its individual members. Dell (1981) in this connection draws attention to 'the shadow side of paradox and strategic therapy'. Children and mentally subnormal individuals make special challenges to us here.

Sixth, do brief forms of treatment which, during the course of treatment, place the therapist in an unassailable position and which rely solely on behaviour change or on changing the family's cognitive set regarding external reality, have subtle, unexpected and perhaps unwelcome side-effects? Removing the need for either a developing *awareness* of its own behaviours and their consequences or *educating* the family to learn to tackle its problems differently in the future means that, as in the widened gap between patient and doctor in physical medicine, the family is kept continually, even if intermittently, dependent upon the services of the therapist when future difficulties arise. Participation, sharing, community self-enhancement, are not easily reconcilable within the brief therapy model. Inherent in the emphasis on the therapist as an unassailable expert is what Downie (1971) describes as a particular kind of impersonal attitude which treats the patient or family as an object. It is again this reification which Dell (1981) describes as the shadow side of strategic therapy.

Seventh, the matter of confidentiality is more complex in family therapy. The demands of third parties such as a court, the agency personnel, the referrer, or members of the family's wider network, may lead to severe pressures on the therapist. Information exchange has been made easier with the growth in the use of computers and data banks and therefore requires even more stringent consideration. Recent legislation allowing clients of certain statutory agencies to have access to automatically processed personal information places extra responsibilities upon therapists working in these agencies to ensure that what is on the file is true and carefully presented. The ethical use of clinical material on video or audio tape for research or teaching remains a problem area in family therapy.

Spiegel (1978) draws attention to the 'age of ethical crises' in which we appear to be living. Perhaps this, if it is so, reflects a desire to retrieve human values and moral concerns from the high-tech influences of science, professionalisation and rapid technical innovation which permeates huge areas of our human experience. In publishing this collection of papers, our aim is to focus attention on the way in which these influences are affecting the family therapy field and the consequent danger to the human values and moral concerns of both family and therapist. We believe that professional workers have to be accountable and that this is best achieved by opening up contentious issues for public debate. It is also a way of closing the gap between the professional expert and the patient recipient and, as Karasu (1981) suggests, mitigating 'the power of professionals as symbolic representations of the inequitable distribution of resources in society' (p. 90).

Our book does not aim to be prescriptive, but attempts to analyse some of the elements of the problems which have to be taken account of when trying to weigh up whether or not a course of therapeutic action is ethically justifiable however pragmatically effective it may be deemed to be. Often, perhaps usually, that which is pragmatically effective for the family is completely in accord with ethical principles, not least because, by being effective, an intervention may be presumed to be helpful in relieving distress, bringing about change or assisting some other goal that is desired by the family and is desirable. The division between effectiveness and acting on principle is complicated but it is arguable that when people apparently choose effectiveness over principle they are really just choosing what is valued short term over what is valued long term and in each case may be valued on moral grounds. All acts are effective – have an effect – but advocates of effectiveness want more, they want what they value soon.

The field of family therapy is still very young, however, and naturally it has concentrated in its past 30 or so years on creating a sound theoretical base and developing techniques that can help shift some of the most intractable relationship problems which have been largely untouched by individual treatment methods. But it is now necessary to examine some of the means used to achieve these laudable ends and to ask some searching questions about the assumptions which lie behind some of our theories, and about the side-effects of some of our techniques.

None of us is very good at conducting self-examination; we are tempted to be too harsh or too lenient. We therefore decided to enlist the help of a group of philosophers and to make use of their specialised expertise in the fields of moral and social philosophy. Coming ourselves from each of the two disciplines of philosophy and family therapy respectively, our hope was to initiate dialogue across the boundary between philosophy and family therapy, so that much could be learnt by both groups.

A concern for the ethics of intervention also implies an interest in the models of 'normality' and 'health' that are important in every psychotherapist's effort to help his or her patient. There are no value-free therapists and no value-free interventions. But for that very reason it is important that therapists bring clearly into focus the models that they *do* use rather than letting them influence their work implicitly. Erickson (1976) made this point powerfully in relating to psychoanalysis. Family therapy, like all other forms of therapy, cannot be morally neutral in its dealings with such a sensitive grouping as the family. It is always at work at the interface between the individual and the corporate, between the personal and the political. As with other forms of therapy, its practitioners have to decide whether their main task is to help families *adjust to* unhappy and conflictual circumstances both within the family boundary and coming at them from outside; or whether their main task is to help families *to change* these circumstances both within the family and within its influencing environment.

Unlike the private setting of individual psychotherapy, family therapists are not usually presented with the more obvious temptations to gratify their own needs at the expense of their patient, yet the more public atmosphere of the family therapy approach, often combined with exposure to video-camera and a one-way screen, may provide a very strong magnetic pull on the narcissistic tendencies of the therapist. Choice of venue, length of treatment, use of the family in 'demonstration interviews' with expert and well-known consultants may all be dictated more by the narcissism of the therapist than the needs of the family.

The family therapist has become a powerful figure. He or she has many more technical tools available than were available a decade ago. But beyond the specific issues raised by the use of more powerful techniques, the family therapist is often in danger of transgressing the boundary between helping the family to define and achieve its goals and dictating what those goals should be. Such dictation may occur very subtly or it may take the grosser form of giving advice under the guise of one's professional authority as to major courses of action which one or more family members should follow. Goldberg (1977) has examined these issues in the therapeutic relationship and emphasises that the major safeguard against abuse of therapeutic power is the concept of true therapeutic partnership. The idea of partnership between therapist and family is as important a safeguard in family therapy as in individual work, but it requires that the therapist view the family as ally not enemy and the relationship between family and therapist as a journey to be walked together not a battle to be won.

In the early days of family therapy's development, therapists were naturally struck by the many differences between family therapy and individual work. Not least among these was the apparent imbalance of power between the single therapist and the family group. Family therapists quickly discovered a need to work in co-therapy pairs, and later in groups and teams in order not only to increase their understanding of family dynamics but also to overcome their own perceived vulnerability. But feeling vulnerable as a therapist is neither good nor bad – it depends how one copes with the feeling and how one makes use of it. Likewise, feeling freed from vulnerability does not automatically increase one's usefulness to the family. It may, I suspect, and often does, create in the therapist a false sense of security and tempt him or her into taking unwarranted risks both in terms of setting over-ambitious treatment goals and utilising over-sophisticated means for achieving them. Using a sledge-hammer to crack a hazelnut can give any of us a great deal of satisfaction, excitement and sense of personal power – but the nut may end up less shattered if we apply a pair of nutcrackers to it instead.

Oddly, the early emphasis of family therapy was very much on equality and partnership. Stress was laid upon the mutual struggle of both parties to develop and grow in their relationships and life goals. The necessity of vulnerability was regarded as a virtue and the old medical model of unequal relationship between doctor and patient was rejected as being an unsound basis for doing family therapy. All this seems now in strong contrast to the extraordinary re-instatement of the medical model by the Milan group of strategic therapists. Here, the relationship between therapist and family is reduced to a detailed *diagnostic* session conducted according to a highly predetermined format, followed, after prolonged *consultation* between the therapist and his expert consultants, by the issuing of a *prescription* to the family, together with a refusal on the part of the therapist to discuss with the family either the meaning of the prescription or its likely effects. We believe that such a shift of emphasis reflects the way in which technique has come to be refined within the family therapy field at the expense of ethical considerations.

This collection of papers opens with critical appraisals of family therapy theory by Watson and Morton, both writing as academic philosophers. Because of the influence that the work of John Bowlby has had on the British practice of family therapy, Watson begins by examining Bowlby's concepts of the environmental stability and lability of biological characteristics; attachment behaviour and maternal deprivation; and the source material for his ideas derived from ethology. Using Strawson's descriptions of the commonplaces of human life and human interaction, Watson examines both Bowlby's theories and the main constructs of general systems theory in the light of Strawson's analysis (for references to Bowlby and Strawson, see chapter 1).

Probably the most important theoretical framework for the family therapist is that of general systems theory. I imagine that few family therapists actually possess enough mathematical knowledge fully to understand the bedrock theory of their discipline, yet most will acknowledge that general systems theory provides the paradigm which enables us to make the leap from intervening in intra-personal events to trying to change inter-personal processes.

Unlike the theory of groups which, especially in Britain, has provided us with a parallel and very fertile source of theoretical knowledge for working with families, general systems theory has tended to deny individual responsibility and to reduce human beings' essential human attributes to a mechanistic and reified model made up of components and processes. Critics have pointed to the changes that come from confusing metaphor with reality. It seemed important therefore to try and tackle these issues head on.

Strawson describes the commonplaces of human life and human interaction, as being made up of the 'interconnections of personal feelings, moral sentiments, social practices, the whole making up a human and social web or network' which provides the essential matrix of human experience. Watson shows that for Strawson, this human experience is essentially interpersonal and 'systemic' and yet it retains an emphasis on the moral commitments, beliefs and intentions of individuals towards each other and the uniqueness of *human* social systems amongst other categories and types of system. Watson sets out to indicate that what is lost through a slavish use of general systems theory may be lost unnecessarily, that conceptions of mental health and mental illness, in the broad senses current in family therapy, might be developed within the framework described by Strawson, paying due attention to our membership of social systems but recognising that such systems are distinct in kind.

Watson's critical analysis of the use which family therapists make of systems theory and the consequences of that use, points up the difficulties involved in the transference of any theory from one field to another. Family therapists use a particularly hybrid range of theories to support their practice. Our textbooks refer to exchange theory, game theory, catastrophe theory, to name but three highly mathematical and scientific frameworks. But what are the criteria by which we may judge the validity of such transfers to the family therapy field? They confront us with problems of accurate interpretation and relevance and, more crucially with the difficulty of being sure that the person doing the transfer is expert enough in *both* fields to ensure a sufficient degree of isomorphy between the nature of the material within the two areas of application.

Morton takes Watson's criticisms of systems theory further. For him systems theory is 'an abomination' and his aim as expressed in chapter 2 is to help family therapists to 'find something that makes more sense'. Morton focusses on causality. He attacks the simplicity with which family therapists frequently describe the linear causal model which they criticise. He distinguishes between truth and utility; it may be that causal attributions are often *true*, though we may not gain much from knowing what the causes are. Morton argues that it is particular events that are causes and effects; that it is usually impossible to determine *the* one cause of an event, given any event is usually related to a mass of other previous events, and that causation does not require determination – thus 'to assign causes to events such as human actions need not be to take them as resulting from some implacable and exceptionless regularity'. Whilst Watson argues that the concepts of systems theory are inadequate for describing human social systems, Morton points out that systems theorists' criticisms of earlier models of causality are themselves inadequate. He suggests that family therapists have misunderstood the meaning of the claims made by a concept of causal-relatedness. But as Carpenter's paper illustrates, a family therapy practitioner would see this issue differently. The family therapist is routinely engaged in a battle with *the family* over *contesting* theories of causality. Morton thinks that part of the picture that family therapists are trying to keep at arm's length is 'something central to the concept of agency: the idea that deliberate actions of human agents are a large part of the exploration of what happens to them.' This, Morton suggests, is 'central to the conception of an autonomous agent' – and autonomy is often what a therapist is helping the individual to try and find. 'Autonomy' is a word that rings strangely in the ears of a family therapist, more accustomed as she is to working with the *limitations* of autonomy. But it is a theme which the philosopher contributors to this volume will not let go; both Lindley and Collier take it up rigorously in later chapters.

Carpenter introduces a range of general issues which are central yet implicit within the family therapy approach. What does it mean for an individual to be treated as part of a family system? Is the individual's behaviour always contingent upon his or her membership of, and position in the system? How far can individuals be held responsible – either causatively or in terms of a 'moral duty' – for the behaviour of other members of the family system? What right does a therapist have to intervene in the lives of family members who are not designated as the patient or client? Is it ethical for the therapist to pursue his work with the family on the basis of a covert understanding of causality which differs sharply from that of the family? Carpenter discusses the relationship between the autonomy of the individual and his or her membership of a family group and without abandoning the most fundamental of all family therapy's premises – that it is the *family* which is the focus of intervention – he points out the many ethical dilemmas involved for the therapist working with family groups where the needs and rights of individual members are in conflict; where there is gross imbalance of power between them; and within a culture, that of Western society, where an aggressive individualism is prized and valued over and beyond the corporate welfare of the group. Carpenter describes the fundamental assumptions and methods of work common to family therapists from a variety of different schools. He discusses the family therapist's notion of causality:

> Family therapists ... assume that causality is complex in family interaction: it is not based on straightforward cause and effect but rather on a series of inter-connected, often simultaneous events, which link up in such a way that it becomes impossible to discern the beginning or an end ... They assume that *every* member of the family is in some measure causally responsible, for everything .... It is the family rather than the individual which is the 'patient'.

He discusses the problems involved in defining the family and placing boundaries around this unit of treatment as well as the even-more-complex problems involved in deciding what is a 'good' family against which the 'sick' family can be measured. He examines the ethical implications of two kinds of technique frequently adopted within the structural model – escalating the symptom and unbalancing the system – both of which increase the stress on non-identified individuals and demand that each owns responsibility for bringing about change. He ends by considering the validity of the systems model itself and the consequences for believing it to be an accurate device for conceptualising the family.

McCluskey describes and discusses an approach to family therapy which she has called theme-focussed family therapy. Much of the impetus behind this way of working arises from concern about the ethical dilemmas apparent in the strategic and structural models. Along with some preliminary work in client-centred family therapy (Levant, 1978), McCluskey's work on the application of existential ideas to family therapy is breaking new ground in its effort to link concepts from humanistic psychology with the family therapy model. Her work is of particular relevance to all those who share a growing concern about the ethical problems apparent in other approaches. McCluskey traces the development from working with individuals to working with families. McCluskey criticises the way in which much family therapy training ignores the need for the therapist to work on himself and his own position in his family of origin. She draws attention to the lack of self-reflexivity in training leading to a very wide gap between family and therapist. McCluskey suggests that far from installing the therapist in a meta-position to the family, the work of therapy revolves around the joint struggle of family plus therapist group to create new and growth-promoting experiences within the sessions. The therapist should avoid adding to the burden of influence, direction and advice with which the family will already be saddled and he or she should create instead an ambience in which family members can take hold of and own what they experience. The therapist is not the ultimate arbiter of meaning; he or she is the enabler and facilitator for family members' search for and creation of new meaning for themselves. In this approach, the family is seen as an equal participant in the struggle both to accept and to change their inner and outer worlds and a fellow seeker after the wisdom required to distinguish the one from the other. The family is not an adversary to be tricked or tamed, but a resource and repository of strength as well as weakness, having things to give as well as the need to receive. McCluskey does not ignore the ethical dilemmas which do arise from this way of working – both those that are generic to all forms of family therapy and those that arise specifically from this approach and she ends her paper with a discussion of these particular problems.

My own paper examines the relationship between feminism and family therapy. I begin by looking at different aspects of emotional development in boys and girls, using psychoanalytic insights to unravel these. In passing, I suggest that, in common with more recent feminist analyses, and because of the way in which feminism has in turn influenced and changed psychoanalysis itself, there is no need to abandon the major constructs of psychoanalytic theory in order to understand the feminine experience, and no need therefore to abandon psychoanalytic insights in order to do justice to feminism in family therapy. The early part of this paper goes on to investigate the relationship between the feminist movement and psychotherapy generally. Feminists have two main attitudes towards psychotherapy: some reject it out of hand as a tool of an oppressive patriarchal system; others have sought ways to recruit it in the service of freeing women from the structures of the society which oppresses them. Some particular issues such as sex bias and sexual stereotyping in psychotherapy and the sexual abuse of female clients are considered. The main purpose of the paper is to examine the relationship between family therapy and feminism and to discuss the ethical concerns with which each confronts the other. Although each can assist the other in understanding the dilemmas of their own system of therapy, I conclude that there are severe limits to the association between the two.

The next three papers focus explicitly on one type of family therapy – the strategic method. Following Stanton (1981) and Olson *et al.* (1983), the term strategic is used here to describe the work of the Brief Therapy Project, Palo Alto; of Jay Haley; of the Brief Therapy Project, New York; of the Milan Associates; of the British work of Cade at the Family Institute, Cardiff and of Campbell, and Draper of the Tavistock Clinic, London. Treacher explores the ways in which family therapy, far from alleviating distress or bringing about constructive change in families, may actually produce a range of harmful effects. Its growing professionalisation, its disparate and unmonitored training of practitioners and its growing emphasis on the technical tasks of the treatment process, all serve to widen the gap between therapist and family. Treacher focuses the bulk of his powerful critique upon the strategic methods of family therapy, and singles out for particular examination the British contributions made to strategic work by Cade and others at the Family Institute, Cardiff. He argues that, if, in the strategic approach, 'therapy is a power struggle between the family and the therapist, then the ideal form of therapy is one that takes place both outside of family members' consciousness and under the therapist's control'. The problem about this, is that, like psychotropic drugs, it does not allow the client or family to gain any understanding of or control over the processes that have caused them to have problems: it effectively decontextualises and depoliticises the human issues involved. Treacher explores the fascinating possibility of there being an unconscious connection between the kind of therapeutic approach which a family therapist feels drawn to use and the kind of personal history, family background and areas of 'pathology' that uniquely belong to him or her. Specifically, Treacher ponders whether it might be possible 'to explain a therapist's attraction to strategic ways of working (which place a premium on distancing therapists from their clients) in terms of their formative experiences in their families of origin?' He raises a question mark over the way in which methods of work are adopted on the basis of therapist preference rather than client need. His ethical objections to strategic forms of therapy are that they are necessarily highly manipulative, to a different degree and to a greater extent than any other form of therapy. By definition, they are covert and non-contractual and involve the dehumanisation of both family and therapist. He challenges the 'method orientation' of most strategic family therapists, which leaves no room for the application of different methods to different family situations; and he ends by pondering the effects that continuous involvement in the tricky, covert and distancing techniques of strategic therapy must have on the personality of the therapist.

Writing as an academic philosopher, Lindley also focuses his attention on the strategic approach to family therapy. He contrasts the truth motive implicit in most communication with the lack of a truth motive in strategic communication. He considers the practices of strategic therapy against the fundamental moral principles of personal autonomy and respect for people. He argues that autonomy and respect for persons are both essential to human dignity and both necessarily imply that humanity has therefore to be treated as an end in itself and never simply as a means. Further, the principles demand that people should not be treated instrumentally or manipulatively, even if for their own good. Interpreted in the strictest sense, there can be no congruence between the principles of respect for persons and their personal autonomy and the practices of strategic therapy. However, Lindley goes on to point out that these two principles are inevitably implausible in their absolutist form and one has therefore to examine how far the conflict with the principles undergirding strategic family therapy is genuine or only apparent. He proposes that these two key ideas should be viewed more as desirable goals than as absolute moral principles. A key question for family therapists then becomes: can 'the goal of maximising respect for people be better promoted by using indirect or devious strategies when it seems appropriate, than by adopting a convention whereby they are avoided except perhaps *in extremis*?'. Lindley goes on to consider two major sources of possible moral dilemma for strategic family therapists: the involvement of family members other than the identified patient in the absence of an accurate reason for doing so and the use of specifically covert and manipulative strategies in treatment. In the first case he argues that, using a liberal interpretation of the moral principles of respect for persons and their autonomy, the involvement of other family members, even without a full explanation to them of the reason why, can usually be justified in terms of the long-term interests of the group. Where the autonomy interests of two parties cancel each other out, 'decisions should rest on other considerations such as justice and utility'. In the second case, Lindley carefully distinguishes between different types of strategic intervention and the degree, meaning and consequences of the deception involved. He concludes that:

> deceptive strategic therapy harms its 'beneficiary' directly in proportion to the importance to the deceived of the desire it frustrates ... for the end of the 'patient' may be not just to become able to cope adequately with life, but to learn to cope whilst not being manipulated or deceived in respect of crucial desires.... If therapists are to maintain ethically acceptable standards of respect for the people they treat, it is important that they use full-blown deceptive strategy, especially over matters about which the client may be supposed to have strong views only as a last resort and not adopt it as anything like standard practice.

Collier again addresses himself to the ethical dilemmas of the strategic approach to family therapy. He begins by discussing the status of the concept 'realism'. Is it actually the case, as Cade (in Cade and Seligman, 1981) maintains, that 'reality is what we choose to define it as'? Collier admits the difficulty involved in defining what is 'real' – but he suggests that strategic family therapists in *their* discussions of reality confuse the distinction

> between dogmatically held beliefs and those that are open to revision; between schematic and fuller conceptions and between the ideas that beliefs can be discoveries about reality and that they are imposed on it for reasons of utility. Clearly, dogmatism and schematism or onesidedness are to be avoided but that in no way commits us to treating beliefs as useful fictions.

Collier carefully distinguishes between different kinds and degrees of deception involved in different strategic techniques. Manipulation can certainly be distinguished from the use of influence, and many of these techniques involve no manipulation. However, manipulation, according to Collier, does occur 'when a person's actions are controlled by getting them to misunderstand the situation'. Manipulation violates the individual's autonomy and 'the harm involved in the violation of someone's autonomy is not merely either the deception or consequences of it adverse to their interests but that the agent is compromised in their actions by a false belief about something close to their heart'. Collier discusses the nature of the reality of systems; are they 'real' or are they metaphoric abstractions? He points out that the effort to diminish the objective reality of systems – to assert idealism over and against realism – has practical effects of the first importance and involves the adoption of an uncompromisingly conservative political stance. To reframe an unacceptable reality removes all impetus to struggle for change – whether this be the individual's own struggle for change or the struggle of a community or society against injustice and oppression. As Collier points out, 'this is the age-old alternative to changing the world; re-interpreting it.'

Kingston takes up the theme raised by Collier – the relationship between the alleviation of intra-familial symptoms and the struggle to change the context in which family and symptoms are embedded. The shift from the individual to the family system is no great shift if we do not make the further shift to the wider contextual supra-system. Family systems may otherwise – and often do – get held responsible for problems that impinge upon them from the environment. Kingston points out that the principle of equifinality is much under-used in family therapy and yet it is a systems concept that frees us to seek out many different starting points for change beyond the family system. Kingston shows how types of occupation, unemployment and low socio-economic status are all major determinants of family structure and family problems. However, knowledge about the ways in which these influences impinge from the supra-system faces the family therapist with two principal dilemmas: first, although such knowledge indicates that the locus of intervention should often be some system other than the family, the therapist usually has limited power to effect change in other systems. Second, although collaboration with other systems may be necessary to bring about changes in the family, the cost of such collaboration may be the therapists' involvement in a process of social control. Kingston challenges the apolitical stance adopted by most family therapists and asks how this can be justified, if the factors which are crucial to the well-being of the family lie in the control of the broader social and political environment?

The book concludes with a paper by Haldane in which he examines the implications for the professional practice of family therapy of some of the earlier discussions in this book. He begins by examining the public positions adopted on ethics by the major caring and health professions – doctors, social workers and psychologists – and then goes on to consider the position adopted by the Association of Family Therapy itself. He discusses the developing awareness of the need to develop guidelines for practice amongst family therapists and he describes how the debate and discussion has grown productively over the years, even though there is still no agreement on the issue of registration amongst either psychotherapists generally or amongst family therapists. Haldane takes up the themes of autonomy, trust, power, responsibility, accountability and consent – themes which appear and reappear in the other papers; and he considers how they might be safeguarded in treatment, training and research. He examines the particular problems connected with confidentiality in family therapy, especially in the light of new legislation which allows retrieval of information about patients by third parties. Teamwork too, practised more and more frequently by family therapists, poses complex problems which cut across the way in which the different disciplines normally relate to one another.

Haldane faces the core of these issues when he ponders 'whether or not ethical codes can or should be introduced to govern or guide the practice of family therapists and how these would influence the work and collaboration of colleagues from different professions working within family therapy teams'. He sees this question as being 'inextricably linked with the question of whether there should be organised a profession of family therapy'. In order for a code of ethics to be effective, it would have to relate to a defined group of professional practitioners – family therapists – who belonged to an organisation that had the power and responsibility to prescribe and monitor the form of training required for the individual to be registered as qualified to practice, as well as defining acceptable standards for the continuation of practice. At present, no such defined group of family therapy practitioners exists and family therapists remain deeply divided as to whether the establishment of such a body is a reasonable goal for them to pursue.

Since 1984, the debate over the professionalisation of family therapy in Britain has become more overt and more widely expressed. Haldane describes and discusses four distinct points of view which he discerns amongst family therapists: that they should organise as a profession; that professionalisation should be resisted; that they should identify, as members of their primary mental health or caring discipline and not with a new profession of 'family therapy'; that a new profession should be organised which embraces all those who can be deemed systems workers whether their interventions are directed towards family systems, or other social or political networks.

Haldane concludes that it will be some time yet before the field of family therapy resolves some of these differences or arrives at an acceptable solution to the problems of the definition of standards for training and practice, the accreditation of workers or the creation of a workable code of ethics for the practice of family therapy. The editors and contributors to this book hope that these papers will at least make a worthwhile contribution to the various aspects of the debate.

I

FAMILY THERAPY, ATTACHMENT THEORY AND GENERAL SYSTEMS THEORY: SEPARATION MAY BE NO LOSS

David Watson

1

To put it discreetly: 'the conceptual framework underpinning family therapy continues to be a matter of some confusion and of considerable debate' (Walrond-Skinner, 1976, p. 11). It would therefore be unwise to attempt an analysis of the theoretical foundation of family therapy, because it doesn't have *one*: 'one is confronted by a "collage" of theoretical standpoints which do not as yet constitute any unified whole' (Walrond-Skinner, 1976, p. 10). This is so despite the fact that where an understanding of theory does not precede its implementation in practice, clients may be harmed, despite the fact that 'theory is not just another gadget which can be used without understanding' (Bateson, 1978, p. 237).

However, that part of the collage derived from 'general systems theory', sometimes reached through 'attachment theory', is widely canvassed as in fact, or in prospect, the most rewarding, and for that reason I shall devote this essay to consideration of what attachment theory and general systems theory have to offer family therapy. The direction of argument is indicated in my title: separation may be no loss.

First step towards this conclusion is to consider a series of 'commonplaces', as elaborated by the philosopher P. F. Strawson, which highlight features of human social life denied in general systems theory; as an account of that social life, the latter is thereby implied to be *reductionist*. To allege reductionism is invariably to suggest that a baby has been thrown out with the bathwater; that baby is the possibility of *therapeutic participation* in human social life, at least on any conception of it which presupposes personal responsibility. And why does *that* matter? Because *ethical* therapeutic intervention is generally thought of as intervention for which the individual therapist is accountable: he or she takes personal responsibility for the conduct of treatment in a morally justifiable manner aimed at ends which he or she chooses to pursue (or assist another to pursue). A reductionist general systems theory is incompatible with ethical therapeutic intervention thus conceived. Strawson's description of 'part of the general framework of human life' (1968, p. 84) introduces no such difficulties, and yet is an account in which the effect of interpersonal relationships on the psychosocial development of individuals may be acknowledged.

2

Interdisciplinary discussion is problematic. Apart from different views of what is of interest, and so of what is worthy of discussion, we must cope with ignorance, not only of what is widely understood and accepted within some discipline not our own, but also of what is controversial, and in what degree. The present discussion raises the latter difficulty in compound form. There is of course the therapist's ignorance of philosophy and the philosopher's ignorance of therapy, but in addition we must cope with the fact that the theoretical writings of therapists inspired by general systems theory, to which we shall turn in due course, draw upon, and present, accounts of theses from a range of disciplines not their own. Further, most readers, myself included, are in no position to assess what has been lost, or gained, in translation from biology, mathematics, engineering, and so on.

What Strawson has to say, he emphasises, 'consists largely of commonplaces' (1968, p. 75). He 'presents a picture... of interconnections of personal feelings, moral sentiments, and social practices; the whole making up a human and social web or network which is capable... of modification but from which we can hardly imagine ourselves... altogether emancipated' (pp. 2–3). The picture is supposed to be familiar to us all. My purpose in repeating Strawson's reminder is to draw attention to what is lost, particularly that which may be assumed to be important to those who would describe themselves as engaged in ethical family therapy, if general systems theory is applied to human social life.

Strawson's picture bears a surface resemblance to that presented by devotees of the application of general systems theory to family life.

> The central commonplace that I want to insist on is the very great importance that we attach to the attitudes and intentions towards us of other human beings, and the great extent to which our personal feelings and reactions depend upon or involve, our beliefs about these attitudes or

intentions... how much it matters to us, whether the actions of other people – and particularly of *some* other people – reflect attitudes towards us of goodwill, affection, or esteem ... contempt, indifference, or malevolence (1968, p. 75).

Think, for example of the difference in personal feelings aroused if someone treads on my toes malevolently, as opposed to accidentally. Such *reactive* attitudes (p. 76), are reactions to the quality of others' wills towards us (p. 84), or, in their analogous generalised form (p. 85ff), towards others, as manifested in their behaviour. They reflect the fact that through the moral life we know as members of human communities (p. 86), we come to think of human beings, others and ourselves, as creatures whose behaviour is normally adequately explained by reference to intentions. Conceived as acting because of beliefs, attitudes or intentions, we are *thereby* conceived as bearers of moral responsibility.

Note acknowledgment of a certain 'circularity' in ordinary inter-personal attitudes. Our attitudes and intentions towards others reflect the attitudes and intentions towards us which we believe to be manifested in their behaviour, just as their actual attitudes and intentions towards us reflect the attitudes and intentions towards them which they believe to be manifested in our behaviour.

Theorists of family therapy also talk of a 'circularity' in human relationships, but, I shall argue later, one cast in terms which leave no work to be done by reference to human will. General systems theory implies that ascription of moral responsibility is based on a misunderstanding of the human condition, and so warrants permanent suspension of ordinary inter-personal attitudes. Reductionist theories of this kind cannot sustain the idea of personal ethical practice with therapeutic intent, both because they make no reference to intent of any kind, and because no personal moral responsibilities are attributable.

Ethical practice with therapeutic intent is part of a human social life in which inter-personal, reactive attitudes are *not* permanently suspended for all relationships. However, within such a social life we might, we do, suspend those attitudes *abnormally*. Focussing on occasions for resentment as a reactive attitude, Strawson discriminates two groups of special consideration which 'might be expected to mollify or modify this feeling or remove it altogether' (p. 77).

First, there are occasions when a phrase such as 'he didn't mean to' is used to invite us to view the agent as one in respect of whom reactive attitudes *are* appropriate, as a fully responsible agent, but one not fully or at all responsible for the injury in question. Second, there are occasions when we are invited 'to suspend our ordinary reactive attitudes towards the agent, either at the time of his action, or all the time' (p. 78).

The first subgroup of this second type of occasion is indicated by phrases such as 'he wasn't himself'. The second subgroup 'allows that the circumstances were normal, but presents the agent as psychologically abnormal – or as morally underdeveloped' (p. 79); he or she is warped or deranged, neurotic or just a child. On occasions such as fall into these subgroups of the second type, we are invited to adopt what Strawson calls the *objective* attitude. Reactive and objective attitudes 'are not altogether exclusive of each other; but they are, profoundly, opposed' (p. 79). Further,

> To adopt the objective attitude to another human being is to see him, perhaps, as an object of social policy; as a subject for what, in a wide range of sense, might be called treatment ... to be managed or handled or cured or trained ... though you may fight him, and though you may talk to him, even negotiate with him, you cannot reason with him (p. 79).

Suspension of inter-personal attitudes is available as a resource: 'we *can* sometimes look with something like the same eye on the behaviour of the normal and the mature ... as a refuge, say, from the strains of involvement' (p. 80). However, since 'our adoption of the objective attitude is a consequence of our viewing the agent as *incapacitated* in some or all respects for ordinary inter-personal relationships' (pp. 82–3), the objective attitude is not usually adopted simply as a matter of convenience. A therapist might suspend ordinary inter-personal attitudes towards his patient or patients, but the suspension 'is profoundly modified by the fact that the aim of the enterprise is to make such suspension unnecessary or less necessary' (p. 90). When this condition is not met, the 'therapist' may be thought of more accurately as a guard.

Strawson's 'commonplaces' have been introduced at length because it is important to have some measure of the revision in our thought and lives required by any theory which commits us to a permanent suspension of all inter-personal attitudes. As Strawson puts it, 'in the absence of any forms of these attitudes it is doubtful whether we should have anything that *we* could find intelligible as a system of human relationships, as human society' (pp. 95–6). There is reason to think that most advocates of general systems theory, and of a family therapy derived from it, have not noticed the price to be paid.[1]

I turn now to discussion of sources for theory in family therapy in order to establish the warrant they give for permanent suspension of all inter-personal attitudes. The first step is to identify the conceptual framework within which such a position could make sense.

3

John Bowlby's contribution to social work practice, particularly those parts of it which must give attention to theories of human growth and development, in contexts significant in family life such as adoption, fostering and bereavement, is commonly acknowledged (Haines, 1975, ch. 5; Kellmer Pringle, 1975, ch. 2; Fahlberg, 1981). So, too, is the value of his 'attachment theory' for a type of family therapy in which 'a family may be seen as a homeostatic system of relationships between a number of individuals at different stages of development. The system is held together by shared (continuing) set goals aimed at adequate termination of proximity-seeking attachment behaviour' (Heard, 1978, p. 74; see also Heard, 1981; and Parkes and Stevenson-Hinde, 1982).

Bowlby's contribution to family therapy is sometimes described as accidental. According to Sue Walrond-Skinner,

> Family therapy in this country has moved a long way since its beginnings, marked by Bowlby's early paper ('The study and reduction of group tensions in the family') ... As is by now well known, this paper holds some claim to have initiated the whole family therapy movement, since it was on reading Bowlby's paper (and misunderstanding the extent to which Bowlby was engaging in conjoint therapeutic work) that Jon Elderkin Bell embarked on his own formative contributions in America (1981, p. 1).

Bell's misunderstanding is in fact compatible with a non-accidental importance for Bowlby's work in the history of family therapy. Indeed, his continued misunderstanding makes more sense in the context of a correct grasp of the conceptual framework implicit in Bowlby's work.

The degree of continuity between attachment theory and general systems theory in the history of ideas is difficult to establish with precision. I turn now to exposition of elements of the conceptual framework for attachment theory because it has limitations in its explanatory power paralleled in family therapy theorising influenced by general systems theory. The continuity exposed, and the difficulties thus carried forward, suggest that family therapy theory has not moved far enough since the beginnings marked by Bowlby's early paper.

I begin my discussion of the views of John Bowlby in tandem with comment on some of those presented by Emmanual Peterfreund (1971). In the Preface to *Attachment and Loss*, vol. 3 (1980), Bowlby declares himself 'much heartened by finding another psychoanalyst who has, independently, adopted a theoretical position almost identical to my own' (p. 2). In Bowlby's judgment Dr Peterfreund was 'influenced by the same scientific considerations' as himself, and each records the judgment that the theoretical frame of reference elaborated by the other is 'strikingly consistent' with his own (Bowlby, 1980, p. 2; see also p. 38, n. 1; Peterfreund, 1971, p. 149, n. 2). In my judgment they're right.

Peterfreund and Bowlby are psychoanalyst clinicians contributing to the development of the theoretical framework for their practice. Their contributions have a common origin, a common aim, and draw on common sources. Each describes the development in his own thinking as stimulated broadly by the desire to be 'more scientific'. The desire is hardly objectionable, but very often turns out to be the first step towards a reductionism arising from the extension of a methodology successful in one field to another in which it is *presumed* appropriate. Peterfreund, in his Foreword, reports himself 'increasingly dissatisfied with psychoanalysis from the standpoint of fundamental science' (1971, p. 9). He therefore set out 'to build new explanatory concepts directly from the empirical clinical phenomena ... and consistent with twentieth century science' (pp. 10–11). However, the clinical phenomena were not reviewed from scratch, but rather giving weight to the fact that 'the psychoanalyst studies a segment of natural phenomena, but so do the physicist, the chemist, and the biologist' (pp. 21–2). This was, he says, 'the beginning of my interest in the general problem of biological organisation and biological order, and in information and systems concepts' (p. 11).

In similar vein, Bowlby reports finding the 'metapsychological superstructure' of psychoanalysis unsatisfactory, and in consequence 'developing a paradigm that... differes from the traditional one in adopting a number of principles that derive from ... ethology and control theory' (p. 38).

In each case, dissatisfaction with traditional explanations of 'clinical phenomena' is dealt with by extension of theory thought to be useful in the study of other natural phenomena. Neither author seriously considers the scope or validity of the source theories, nor questions the scope of their useful extension to explain 'clinical phenomena',[2] although Peterfreund at least emphasises that the framework he commends cannot conceptualise 'sensations, feelings, urges, thoughts, fantasies', which he describes as all 'affects', components of 'the subjective character of human experience', the experience of which, he says, 'constitute consciousness' (p. 35).

The questions of scope are important for the allegation of reductionism and commitment to permanent suspension of all inter-personal attitudes. The disciplines from which our present authors draw satisfaction, in their pre-imperial forms, place their practitioners in relationship with non-natural phenomena (as does information theory), or with non-human natural phenomena (as does zoology), or with phenomena in which human beings feature as supra-or sub-systems (as in biochemistry). In each case their practitioners do not engage in a relationship with a person, they do not deal with actual or would-be members of a moral community who might be assigned moral responsibility. Inter-personal attitudes would therefore always be out of place. In the human sciences, attitudes may themselves be studied with detachment (Strawson, 1968, p. 96), but practitioners of therapy necessarily engage in a relationship between themselves, a person, and another who is, or is to be, a person; permanent suspension of inter-personal attitudes in this kind of context may be inappropriate because it takes no account of the place of such attitudes in the explanation of *human* behaviour, and so in its modification. But in that case these source disciplines may make little or no useful contribution to understanding normal (inter-personal) human social life, even if they are relevant to understanding the non-social context of our lives, since 'in respect of man's anatomical and physiological equipment a continuity in structure with that of other species is unquestionable' (Bowlby, 1969, p. 40).

Peterfreund urges us to take 'the decisive step of viewing the mind of man in a larger biological and evolutionary context' (1971, p. 40); Bowlby announces that 'at last the principles of a unified behavioural science are begining to emerge' (1969, p. 38); but as Bowlby recognises, 'it would be naive to assume that such theory can already solve behavioural problems of the degree of complexity that confront the clinician, or even that it will do so soon' (1969, p. 41). Further, the differences between human and other behaviour may not reduce to complexity, but be in addition, and most significantly, a difference in (conceived) kind, as Strawson's 'commonplaces' imply. In that case the 'decisive' step simply prepares the way for reductionism and the permanent suspension of inter-personal attitudes.

Let us now turn to some details of Bowlby's revised framework for understanding human behaviour.

Environmentally stable and environmentally labile characteristics

Any biological character that in its development is little influenced by variations of environment is termed 'environmentally stable'; any that in its development is much influenced by such variations is termed 'environmentally labile' (1969, pp. 38–9).

Environmentally stable and labile characteristics form a continuum: 'every biological character, whether it be morphological, physiological, or behavioural, is a product of the interaction of genetic endowment with environment' (p. 38). Examples of stable characteristics are morphological ones such as colour of eyes, and behavioural characteristics such as the nest-building of birds; examples of labile characteristics are body weight, and behavioural characteristics such as show-jumping and playing the piano (p. 39).

Bowlby presents as central to human social life what he would classify as environmentally stable 'patterns of human behaviour, often very intensely motivated, that result in mating, in the care of babies and young children, and in the attachment of young to parents' (p. 39). These characteristics, in most circumstances, he says 'are of obvious survival value' (p. 39):

> the more carefully an individual is studied the clearer it becomes that almost every detail of its structure, whether morphological, physiological, or, in the case of animals, behavioural, is adapted so that survival of that individual and its kin is secured in that environment (p. 53).

Or rather, given developments in Neo-Darwinian theory, 'the ultimate outcome to be attained is always the survival of the genes an individual is carrying' (p. 56).

We might note some ambiguity in the claim. Is almost every detail of an individual's structure adapted so that in a particular environment it, or the genes it is carrying, might survive, or *must* survive?

In the former case it would not follow that inter-personal attitudes are appropriately suspended, because the individual may retain intentions and attitudes reactive to those of others, who might in turn adopt reactive attitudes to him. Survival of the individual is a necessary condition of him or her having intentions, but it does not follow that survival of that individual, its kin or the genes it is carrying is the ultimate outcome at which it aims, or indeed is an outcome at which it aims; all that follows is that it *might* be, though the aim is more readily concevied as instrumental, necessary in our pursuit of more plausibly ultimate aims connected with moral, social and political commitments. And if that's what our survival is devoted to, inter-personal attitudes are most appropriate, since almost all such commitments are expressed in behaviour manifesting good or ill will towards some other people.

In the *latter* case, which I think a more plausible interpretation, general systems theory, or at least its Neo-Darwinian source, reveals itself as a determinism, and shows why, if accepted, it warrants permanent suspension of inter-personal attitudes: human beings are no longer agents, but mere means to genetic outcomes not under our will, and summarised as 'reproductive success'.

Attachment behaviour

The environmentally stable patterns of human behaviour that result in mating, in the care of babies and young children, and in the attachment of young to parents (1969, p. 39) include what Bowlby calls 'attachment behaviour' and, serving a complementary function, 'caregiving'. Attachment behaviour is conceived as:

> any form of behaviour that results in a person attaining or retaining proximity to some other differentiated and preferred individual ... the behaviour may consist of little more than checking by eye or ... in certain circumstances, ... following or clinging to the attachment figure may occur and also calling or crying, which are likely to elicit his or her caregiving (1980, p. 39).

'The goal of attachment behaviour is to maintain an affectional bond' (p. 42), and the point of that, as we have seen, is to secure the survival of the genes the individual is carrying through the survival of that individual or its kin. Thus 'the many forms of emotional distress and personality disturbance, including anxiety, anger, depression and emotional detachment, to which unwilling separation and loss give rise' (p. 39) may be explained, and a distinction drawn between healthy and pathological behaviour.

> During the course of healthy development attachment behaviour leads to the development of affectional bonds or attachments (p. 39) ... Psychopathology is regarded as due to a person's psychological development having followed a deviant pathway (p. 41) ... healing processes, we know, may take a course which in time leads to full, or nearly full, function being restored ... processes of mourning may take a course that leads in time to more or less complete restoration of function, namely, to a renewal of the capacity to make and maintain love relationships; or they may take a course that leaves this function impaired (p. 43).

According to Bowlby, an individual is healthy only if he or she has the capacity to make and maintain 'love relationships'; attachment behaviour, to be functional, must elicit caregiving. Health is thus not an attribute of any individual in isolation, but of an individual in a particular relationship, and in that sense a *social* phenomenon.

The 'love relationships' necessary to health are those which may be expected to secure the survival of the genes the individuals are carrying, through the survival of those individuals or their kin; healthy development includes development of attachment behaviour functional in relation to the outcome described; we might add 'given *whatever* social arrangements are in place'. It would be a misunderstanding to think Bowlby's theoretical framework has more specific social implications. Beyond genetic survival, anything goes: all social arrangements in this or any other society remain outside the critique implied by this conception of health. Beyond relationships functional for genetic survival, Bowlby's conception of health commits him neither to reactionary nor revolutionary social arrangements. Even so, the conception is apparently normative: some critique is implied: genetic survival, at least, is valued, and arrangements which facilitate this outcome commended.

But this, too, is a misunderstanding. The stable patterns of behaviour in question, and their outcomes (like any stable or labile pattern, for Bowlby) are not conceived as *chosen* by the individuals, nor as valued by them. Within the theoretical framework Bowlby has developed, we are invited to conceive of human social life as determined by patterns sustained over generations only if a means to genetic survival; this conception is incompatible with that of people engaging in inter-personal relationships, adopting the reactive attitudes conveyed from generation to generation as appropriate in those relationships. In commending the framework he develops, Bowlby invites us to adopt a thoroughgoing objectivity of attitude in presenting an account of human social life minus the context necessary for commitment of any kind, even to genetic survival, and so also minus the context necessary for use of a normative conception of health. In advocating social conditions which promote health, Bowlby is inconsistent with the framework he develops, as one might expect a *person* to be.

Within Bowlby's framework, human social life has one outcome, though no purposes. The contending framework I have introduced allows a rich array of purposes a person might pursue. Strawson, describing a central feature of that contending framework, refers us to 'the very great importance that we attach to the attitudes and intentions towards us of other human beings, and the great extent to which our personal feelings and reactions depend upon, or involve, our beliefs about these attitudes and intentions' (1968, 75). Much, if not all of that importance comes from the part those others may play in assisting or hindering us in our purposes. This is true whether our purpose be to promote our own interests, the interests of others, joint interests, or the interests of a collectivity of which we are a member. The social web of personal feelings, moral sentiments and social practices described by Strawson (p. 2), is also a web of purposes.

Adapting Bowlby's terminology, within the contending framework we may conceive 'love relationships' more broadly as the inter-personal relationships, necessary to health, in which individuals collaborate in pursuit of their own, others', joint and fellow members' purposes. We thereby also adopt a normative conception of health, and might consistently advocate social conditions which create opportunities for purposive behaviour. It is more common to adopt a narrower conception and to advocate more restrictive social conditions, taking the view that some pursuits are unhealthy, though at this point 'health' seems far from home: the issues seem detached from conceptions of human nature and development, and purely moral.

If we recognise an array of purposes, we do not thereby deny the occurrence of behaviour functional in the way Bowlby describes, and in the form he calls 'attachment behaviour'. The point is simply that human beings normally form attachments of other kinds, independently of their relation to genetic survival, in the web of pursuits which is a constituent of human social life as now portrayed. Our loss, sadness and depression when such inter-personal relationships end, in part may be explained by reference to memories of earlier purposes achieved and present purposes frustrated; recovery waits upon renewed purpose in the context of those inter-personal relationships available to us. Following Strawson, we might say that only special considerations, which present the agent as psychologically abnormal or morally undeveloped, require resort for explanation to 'attachment behaviour' functional in the way Bowlby describes.

Maternal deprivation

In *Child Care and the Growth of Love* (1953, second edition 1965; all references to the second edition), Bowlby describes a particular component of 'attachment behaviour' as underlying 'the development of character and of mental health' (p. 13).

> ... what is believed to be essential for mental health is that an infant and young child should experience a warm, intimate, and continuous relationship with his mother (or permanent mother-substitute – one person who steadily 'mothers' him) in which both find satisfaction and enjoyment.... A state of affairs in which a child does not have this relationship is termed 'maternal deprivation' (pp. 13–14).

In these intimate domestic events, says Bowlby, lie the origins of mental disturbances (p. 16): anxiety, excessive need for love, nervous disorders and instability of character; effects, amongst others, which constitute an incapacity to make relationships with other people (p. 14), and constitute underdevelopment of those physical, mental and social capacities necessary to deal with his physical and social environment effectively (p. 84).

It can hardly be disputed that a person lacks mental health if he or she entirely lacks the capacity to make any relationships with other people. However, Bowlby's interest is not in that conditon, but in the incapacity to make relationships which are *effective*. By what criterion 'effective'? Particular instances of the disturbances described may be identified only by reference to outcomes in relation to which they are too much or too little (fear, need for love, nervous disorder, steadfastness of character) to be effective as a means.

In this early text, the outcomes in question are already not quite the purposes of persons. Thus,

> ... one of the principal social functions of an adult is that of parenthood ... (and) it is seen how children who suffer deprivation grow up to become parents lacking the capacity to care for their children, and how adults lacking this capacity are commonly those who suffered deprivation in childhood. This vicious circle is the most serious aspect of the problem ... (p. 79).

Many people choose to be parents, and want to fulfil any obligations to their children which may enable them, in turn, to be caring parents. However, neither the social functions of an adult, nor the incapacities, or capacities, he or she may cause are necessarily outcomes he or she intended. The former are Bowlby's focus, and in his view best accounted for by biological principles.

Thus mental health consists in possession, and mental illness in the lack, of the capacity to form relationships with other people effective in bringing about parenthood of the kind in which the capacity to form such relationships is transmitted. Since capacities are confirmed in action, we can never be sure that those who are childless are not a little mentally ill.

Bowlby's advocacy of social (environmental) reforms (ch. 8), so that mental illness may be reduced, his talk of 'problems', 'suffering' and 'vicious' circles, conveys the impression of a normative conception of mental health. But the foundations for such a conception are already undermined. What is advocated is only what is believed to be 'natural'. Speaking of 'deprived' children he says:

> It is exactly the kind of care which a mother gives without thinking that *is* the care which they have lacked ... again the comparison with physical health brings home the truth. A mother provides the needed food substances in her own milk in exactly the right combination without having to make a chemical analysis and work to a formula. It is only when nature's gifts are lacking that science must study what they are in order to make the best shift it can to replace them (p. 18).

Note that what a mother provides 'without thinking' is twice said to be *exactly right*, while it is also admitted that sometimes it is not. Of the two conditions found in nature, how is the *right* condition identified? Bowlby goes on to add that 'the normal mother can afford to rely on the prompting of her instincts' (p. 20). As we have seen, it turns out that this is because the stable patterns of behaviour in question are adapted to genetic reproduction through the survival of the individual or his or her kin; this outcome is the measure of what is exactly right provision. The question unanswered is *why* science must make the best shift it can to replace 'nature's gifts' when they are lacking. The reproduction of parenting in a form more likely to lead to the reproduction of parenting is not self-evidently valuable; the normative core of this conception of mental health rings hollow, as indeed it must, for a social world in which inter-personal attitudes have no place is one in which outcomes are never valued purposes.

In this section I have been concerned to represent the views of those who believe that:

> A long-awaited theoretical breakthrough has been achieved by analytical biology and control theory, which together have elucidated the basic principles that underlie adaptive goal-directed behaviour ... at last the principles of a unified behavioural science are beginning to emerge (Bowlby, 1969, pp. 37–8).

Such theories invite us permanently to suspend inter-personal attitudes because they invite us to conceive human behaviour within an explanatory framework which leaves no room for human purpose; strictly, it leaves no room for persons; the presumption seems to be that if there were any, they'd probably die out.

Let us now turn to current theorising in family therapy derived from 'the systems framework'. The work discussed is intended to be representative, and my aim is to show that the warrant for suspension of inter-personal attitudes, given by general systems theory, is taken up in accounts of family therapy derived from it.

4

In family therapy texts the first step in applying general systems theory in the explanation of human social behaviour is introduction of the idea of 'a family system'. Thus, at an early stage in her text, Gill Gorell-Barnes explains:

> the idea of a family system is based on the notion of the organisation of pattern over time ... Family pattern is made up of inter-personal relationships involving peiple with individually specific conditions and past histories, living in a particular social network in a particular culture (1984, p. 5).

General systems theory, so far, seems to offer a theoretical framework which leaves Strawson's 'commonplaces' undisturbed. But if we draw closer we begin to see that this is not so. Walrond-Skinner introduces the components of the conception of a system which provide a framework for applying the theory to the family group. It will not be necessary to comment on all five components to draw attention to the extent to which the accounts follow the reductionist tradition identified in the source texts discussed, a heritage which would warrant permanent suspension of inter-personal attitudes.

Wholeness

A system is a *whole* in the sense that:

> its objects (or components) and their attributes (or characteristics) can only be understood as functions of the total system. A system is not a random collection of components, but an interdependent organisation in which the behaviour and expression of each component influences and is influenced by all the others ... interest lies in the transactional processes that take place *between* the components of a system and between their attributes .... It would not be possible to gain much understanding of chess, for example, simply by looking at the pieces; one would need to examine the game as a whole, and to take note of how the movement of one piece affects the position and meaning of every other piece on the board. Applied to the family group, the theorist is concerned with this quality of non-summativity, by which the nature of the transactional processes between family members transcends the activity of individual family members themselves when viewed in isolation (Walrond-Skinner, 1976, p. 12).

The reductionist heritage is already evident: first, in the easy-going claim that the behaviour and expression of each component influences and is influenced by all the others. When kinds of influence remain undiscriminated, all may be taken to be of one kind. This they may be, but this must be argued for, not drifted towards. Understanding family life may require a theory which discriminates between influences, and in particular between influences of the kind which engage thought and the kind which do not. The language of 'influence' facilitates reductionism by presenting consciousness as of no special significance in the explanation of human social life.

Our consciousness makes the analogy between the transactions of family life and a game of chess of dubious value. The 'influence' of the movement of one piece on the potential movements of the others is entailed by the rules which constitute the game. Family life may in some sense be rule-governed, but the range of behaviour possible for family members is not settled by the behaviour of others as a matter of deduction from such rules. If you move other than within the rules of chess, you cease to play chess; if you behave other than others expect, demand or think justified, you do not thereby cease to participate in the life of your family: the family may decide to go on in a new way.

What are we to make of the idea that the nature of the transactional processes between family members transcends the activity of individual members viewed in isolation? There must be more to it than the point that an analysis of the activity of individuals in isolation must be blind to transactional processes between individuals. As we shall see when we come to what is said about causality, the point may be that no act of an individual member can be, as it were, first cause.

Protection and growth

A system is conceived as capable of self-protection and growth.

> Homeostasis is made possible by the use of information coming from the external environment and being incorporated into the system in the form of feedback. Feedback triggers the system's regulator which by altering the system's internal condition, maintains homeostasis. Homeostasis is ... a functional, protective mechanism. Homeostasis does not imply something set and immobile, a stagnation. It means a condition – a condition which may vary, but which is relatively constant. Clearly, the healthy, functional family system requires a measure of homeostasis in order to survive ... to maintain stability and security within its physical and social environment. It is only when these mechanisms over-function that the system becomes fixed and dysfunctional in its rigidity ... The same applies to the family, which, as a system requires either inter-personal or intra-personal homeostatic mechanisms in order to operate effectively (Walrond-Skinner, 1976, pp. 14–15).

Reductionism again is evident, in the application of the central heating system metaphor to family life, with its consequent failure to consider the significance of differences between a thermostat and a person identified as a patient. The phenomenon of homeostasis is a 'mechanism' in each case, and, one might add I suppose, that suspension of inter-personal attitudes is thought to be as appropriate towards those people who figure in its occurrence in one setting as it is towards those bi-metallic strips which figure in its occurrence in another.

Further, a non-normative conception of health, consistent with that identified in source works, seems to be employed. The healthy family is apparently that which is 'functional' and 'effective', and which furthers the family's 'own unique goals' (p. 17). What are these goals? In an example, homeostatic *overfunction* is identified where a daughter continues to replace mother as father's constant companion and support beyond the time necessitated by mother's hospitalisation. Why this threatens the survival of the family, except because of the *beliefs* its members hold, is not said. But in that case homeostatic overfunctioning in families is different in kind from that in central heating systems. Perhaps the thought is that the daughter's behaviour, as a rule, would be less effective in securing the survival of the genes the individual is carrying than would the conventional relationships called 'healthy'. That at least would echo source texts.

Causality

In the classical model of pure science, causality is understood as being linear ... if one is working from the premise that many significant aspects of the system can only be understood by examining the system as a whole, aetiology has to be considered from a different point of view. For example, a family may see Johnny and his delinquency as the 'cause' of their distress, forgetting that Johnny's stealing may be reactive to his mother's emotional absence, which may be reactive to her husband's harsh handling of Johnny ... In G.S.T., causality is viewed as a circular process. It is ... without beginning or end, and thus any attempt by the therapist to transfer responsibility for how the family's problem started from one part of the system to another, is as inappropriate as the family's own blame game, which focusses on the identified patient as the source of the difficulty (Walrond-Skinner, 1976, p. 21).

Adam Morton's contribution to this volume discusses causality at greater length, but some comment is appropriate here. First, attempts to isolate the cause of a particular effect are compatible with recognition of that cause as itself having a cause. Furthermore, a cause may turn out to be a cluster of phenomena whose interaction produces the effect. And of course, what the family forget in their explanation of John's stealing they may be reminded of, and accept without adopting general systems theory. The Strawsonian account recognises such interaction while discriminating it from interactions outside human social life.

Second, the idea that individual responsibility is incompatible with recognition that individual behaviour is always reactive to the behaviour of others is unsupported and implausible. It might be plausible within a reductionist framework which was deterministic, in which 'mechanisms', 'reactions' and 'influences' were all of a piece outside our control, as in general systems theory. Within such a framework a little boy is presumed to be *driven* by something, his mother's 'emotional absence' is suggested, but that presumption is not warranted merely by the fact that his behaviour is reactive; nor, then, is suspension of inter-personal attitudes warranted; given the injury he intended, resentment might be in order.

Purpose

> Organic and social systems are always goal-oriented and purposive.... When the family therapist joins the family system he does so in order to assist in redirecting it towards the achievement of its own unique purpose (pp. 21–2).

This particular passage echoes those of our source texts which claim the relevance of theories in biology. And if the outcome of development for an organic system in its environment of adaptedness is genetic survival, then at what does the family therapist aim? Presumably, at parenting likely to ensure the survival of the genes the individuals are carrying. This is the measure, not usually made explicit, of the essential requirements of child rearing.

In the discussion of this section I do not mean to suggest that popular applications of general systems theory or its component concepts are without critics. Dell (1982) and Keeney and Sprenkle (1982) offer critical discussions of use made of the concept of homeostasis and the continued commitment to dualism, respectively, but these and otherwise useful critical discussions, continue to deny personal responsibility and so remain reductionist in the sense identified.

5

It has been my intention to expose the deterministic reductionism of accounts of the theory and method of family therapy derived from attachment theory or from general systems theory. Since each denies sense to the language of individual moral responsibility, individuals who see their practice as derived from either should not present themselves as responsibly engaged in ethical therapy. It may be that they are in fact engaged in ethical therapy, but then their practice is not consistently derived from attachment theory or general systems theory, but only obscured by association with it.

2

WHO STARTED IT? REMARKS ABOUT CAUSATION

Adam Morton

1

We have many reasons for wanting to know why something happens. Sometimes we can express the answer to a 'why?' question by giving a cause of the event or phenomenon in question. Perhaps that is the traditional way of giving the answer. But it is clearly not always the only or best way of giving the answer. Family therapists are sometimes quite vehement in the repudiation of the concept of cause. 'We don't ask what causes behaviour,' they say. 'We look for the systems of interacting motive and behaviour by which groups of people maintain social patterns' (see Hoffman, 1971; Maruyama, 1968; Wender, 1971; Gurman, 1981). They see the use of too simple causal vocabulary as tied to a number of things they are committed to avoiding; psychological determinism, judgmental moralising, and above all the choice of an individual as the deviant whose behaviour is to be brought into line. My aim is to give a sort of an underpinning to the family therapists' rhetoric, a fairly general way of saying when cause is a helpful notion and when it gets in the way. Family therapists often rely on gestures towards general systems theory for this. I think general systems theory is an abomination, and I'd like to help them find something that makes more sense. Below I set out the situation, draw some tidy and complacent conclusions, and then try to dig up some of the more subtle issues I have missed.

2

Examples

(a) the quarrel: A and B are having a long drawn-out fight. A has asked B to wake her up in the morning. B walks into her room at the required time, says 'Good Morning', puts a cup of tea beside the bed and goes off to work. When A eventually wakes, very late, she takes the cup of stale tea and pours it into the petrol tank of B's motorbike. B takes the bike to his dance lessons that evening but 100 yards from the house the engine dies. Suspecting sabotage, he walks back to the house and has it out with A. She confesses, proudly, and says why he started it. He explains why *she* had really started it: the morning before she had turned off the alarm clock before it had had a chance to wake him. She says...

(b) needling: C's family plans to go on a trip to a wildlife park. C finds this boring, would like not to go, but cannot simply refuse without exposing herself to her father's anger. So she exploits this anger, via his pride in appearances, telling him very early in the day that his shaving is sloppy, suggesting after breakfast that he change his shirt, and then soon before they are due to leave pointing out to him that the coat he was planning to wear has a coffee stain on the lapel. Then, just on the point of departure, she asks her mother to tell him that the car needs washing – someone has written 'clean me' in the dust on its side. Her mother, not having noticed the morning's needling, says bluntly 'that car's embarrassing: you should give it a wipe before we go'. C's father explodes at his wife, she retires in tears, and the trip is off.

(c) equilibrium: D and E are academics who admire each other's work. When either one publishes anything the other reads it at once and absorbs its conclusions into his way of thinking. D and E both write books which appear at about the same time. Both books are reviewed in the same issue of the *Times Higher Education Supplement* by F, a figure in the establishment of their subject to whom both D and E have mixed feelings. They admire his intelligence and learning but think that his view of the subject is old fashioned and unimaginative, and as a result they are not sure how much to trust his judgment. F praises D's book and dismisses E's. D and E then have a problem in their attitude to F: if his judgment is bad then his praise of D is devalued, and if his judgment is good then his criticism of E is justified. D rereads F's favourable review of his book and concludes that the praise is really pretty stupid: it is all for the wrong things.

3

Easy analysis

In all of these cases there are dangers in talking complacently of what caused what. A and B in (a) are victims of, as well as illustrations of, some of the dangers. They think that they can ask what action of which one of them caused their quarrel and draw useful conclusions and moral judgments from it. But they cannot. It is clear – from my telling of their story, which either of them would challenge – both that knowing causes is not by itself going to make them understand their situation, and that the very search for causes is tied to a set of childish and unhelpful moral concepts. Each wants to know that actions of the other, caused the quarrel in such a way that blame will fall on the other, who will then be obliged to be contrite and, in a way, to submit.

(b) prevents us from drawing too-easy morals from this, though. In (b) C does cause her parents' quarrel, and does cause the expedition to be aborted. Moreover some of the pre-requisites for simple blame are met, though what follows from this may depend on the details of the situation. What (b) shows is that whether or not it is very helpful or enlightening, a causal attribution may sometimes be *true*. Of course this is true of (a) too: there are truths about cause and effect there too. And in both cases much more detail would have to be given to show the relation between these causes and the underlying patterns and laws.

(c) is a standard case of a self-sustaining pattern of behaviour. D and E act on each other in such a way as to maintain their roles as reinforcers of each other's self-esteem. As in (b), each particular act can be given a cause and has among its effects other acts. D's conclusion about the review of his book is caused by his reading the review of E's book, and has as an effect D and E agreeing to a lowered opinion of F. But as in (a) the basic principles behind the pattern of action ('what is really going on', 'what the actions mean') are missed by lists of individual actions and their causes. In this case these basic principles amount to a kind of homeostasis: there is a target situation which is maintained by a variety of means, some of them in fact improvised from occasion to occasion. Some of the insights lost by a purely causal description are thus: that equilibrium would have been restored by some other means if the one taken had not been available, that had various other similar disruptions occurred 'the system' would have responded in a generally similar way, and most importantly that had the mutual dependence of the two people's pride not taken the form it did, few of these causal relations would have been found.

But it is important to see that very similar conclusions can be drawn in a case like (a) which is not one of homeostasis. As I have described (a) it could equally be part of a continuing and repeating pattern essential to the relationship between A and B or an isolated incident between people who do not know each other very well. I meant it to be ambiguous in this way. Suppose that A and B do not know each other well and nothing similar happens again. Then although there is no system to speak of and no self-sustaining pattern, it is still the case that causal concepts can only give a shallow understanding of what is going on. For knowing what previous offence caused each succeeding escalation tells you nothing about why it did so, or why it caused this form or degree of escalation.

This last remark raises issues to which I shall return later (in section 5). For the moment, here are three fairly harmless preliminary conclusions.

(i) Causes are not laws: understanding a phenomenon involves having laws of some generality which apply to it. They very rarely have the form 'A causes B'. More often, they have the form 'if something of kind A happens then under conditions C something of kind B will happen (may happen, has probability P of happening, . . .)'. The causal statements can sometimes be derived from the laws; the reverse is very rare.

(ii) Similar events have different causes: the fact that we apply the same label to two events, or even that they clearly have some deep and natural similarity, does not mean that they will have as causes or effects other events which we can apply the same labels to or find the same similarities in. To state the causes of an event may thus tell one very little about other similar events.

(iii) Causes give few ifs: when you know that C caused E you usually still don't know what would have happened *if* C had not happened, what could have prevented E (i.e. what, if anything, would have had to have been different earlier *if* E had not happened), what was possible and what was excluded once C had happened (i.e. what truths of the form '*if* C then F is possible' are true).

These conclusions are meant to be consistent with the general principle: usually there are causes, but you often don't learn much by knowing them.

4

What philosophers say

My examples have been deliberately focussed on human relations. And also, deliberately, have not been examples from psychotherapy. But the points they illustrate could easily be made with examples about completely non-human things. They represent quite general worries about the usefulness of the concept of causation. It is thus not surprising that the philosophical literature contains a number of parallel themes.

Philosophical discussion of causality is focussed, to an almost ridiculous extent, on Hume's attempt to construct in empiricist terms a definition of causality consistent with eighteenth-century science. Hume's account states clearly several assumptions which were taken for granted until quite recently (with the exception of Russell, 1917, largely ignored at the time).

The two main ones are (a) that causality holds between kinds of events, e.g. between poisonings and deaths, or impacts and motions, and (b) that when there is a cause there is a deterministic law of nature ('C's are always followed by E's'), so that given the cause the effect has to follow. Any theory constructed around these assumptions is a version of the Bad Old Picture of causation.

We have escaped from the Bad Old Picture now. Now we think of it as a perverse sandwich of a metaphysics that accompanied Newtonian mechanics spread over a misunderstanding of common sense. I give a brief sketch below of the direction of the escape. It is worth remarking, though, that common sense has been to some extent captured by the Bad Old Picture, in that when people fear that giving causes for human actions reduces people to machines or when they think that 'every event has a cause' expresses determinism they are assuming that the bad old assumptions must be built into any understanding of causation.

Our escape is based on three crucial realisations. The first is that it is *particular* events that are causes and effects (Davidson, 1980, chs 6–10). That is, although one can ask 'what causes the common cold?' and be answered 'infection with a virus', this is really shorthand for 'episodes of infection with a virus cause instances of cold symptoms'. This makes a difference when events of some kind can have a variety of causes: *this* fire can be caused by lightning, that one by a match, that other by spontaneous combustion, and so on. Causes and kinds usually come apart like this in social situations: this quarrel was caused by this situation, this other by that other. Two consequences of the first realisation are worth stressing. (i) different instances of the same types of event can be related in different ways. Some strikings cause lightings, but some lightings cause strikings, too. (You see my match light, and as a result decide to light yours, and so strike it.) One drop in temperature can cause a change in the heating system and another drop in temperature be an effect of such a change. This is important because it shows one way in which cause need not be 'linear': the direction of causation between two kinds of event can typically go either way, for example in any homeostatic and most social situations. (ii) what causes and what is caused are typically *changes* in the states of things. It is not the temperature that causes the state of the heating system, but the change in temperature that causes the change in the state of the heating system.

The second crucial realisation is the ultimate hopelessness of talking about *the* cause of an event (Mill, 1843; Woodfield 1976). Any event is related to so many other previous events, without many of which it could not have occurred, that picking out any of them as *the* cause is simply pointless. For example: A man chokes on a piece of meat and dies. He would not have choked if he had not drunk too much, and he would not have died had he not been grossly overweight and had his circulation not been poor. Immediate causes of death are his choking and his inability to survive loss of oxygen for more than a few seconds; more distant causes are his drunkenness and his poor circulation; yet more distant causes are his lack of exercise, his carnivorous habits, and the absence from the restaurant of anyone knowing the Heimlich manoeuvre. It is hard enough to say which of all these to count as causes at all, without having also to find among them a single pre-eminent one to label *the* cause. In fact, there are three notions here: the causal relation, which holds between an event and all the events which can count as causes of it, the idea of a precipitating cause, and the idea of a main or central cause. All three are vague, but they are different.

The main importance of this point is that it underlines the parochiality of our concept of cause. We have constructed in our commonsense a delicate and somewhat mysterious mixture of ideas about causal necessity, about necessary and sufficient conditions, and about various other things, which is our concept of cause. Other times and other places have had other mixtures: there is no easy transcription of the old Greek 'aitia' – as in Aristotle's idea of causal order – into our causal vocabulary, in part because it focuses on ecological and teleological examples which our concept, however well or badly it handles them, certainly does not take as central (Woodfield, 1976).

The third crucial realisation is that causation does not require determination: that often one event causes another, although the second event could have failed to follow the first. My car goes over a pothole and disintegrates into a pile of a million pieces. But it could have gone over that pothole at that speed and been undamaged; it just so happened that the moment of impact coincided with all sorts of random things happening, and so it collapsed. But for all that the running over the pothole is still the cause of the disintegration. Strangely enough, it took the indeterminism of the quantum world to bring this point home: a photon meets an atom and as a result a variety of energy transitions and photon emissions can take place; whichever one does occur is obviously caused by the absorbtion of the photon, although that event did not make it inevitable. But the point is perfectly general (Anscombe, 1975).

This separates causal from mechanistic thinking. To assign causes to events, such as human actions, need not be to take them as resulting from some implacable and exceptionless regularity. Moods and emotions, beliefs and desires, can cause behaviour, but they need not determine the behaviour they cause.

5

A paradox?

It seems that we have found our way to a fairly comfortable conclusion, into which both the intuitions of therapists and the analyses of philosphers may be fitted. Causation is a fragile concept, and its extension is vague, but events often have other events as causes; when these events are human actions causation is rarely deterministic or linear, and knowing causes will give you very little of what you need to understand an action. The villain, then, the idea that we must keep at arm's length, is not causality itself but the Bad Old Picture, whose effects are as harmful in physics as in psychology.

I think all this is true. But I cannot suppress the thought that it leaves something out. In particular, the perversity of asking for causes in a case like (a) of section 2 does not yet seem adequately described.

Here is one thing that seems to have been left out. Consider again the two people, A and B, of the example. Each thinks that the other started the vendetta, meaning by this that the other did some deliberately quarrelsome thing which set off the chain of retributions. Quite ignoring the foolishness of thinking that such a first cause would in any way justify the subsequent reactions, their attitude still seems perverse. The perversity cannot lie in their thinking that some action could have been a cause of the quarrel, for if what I have been saying is right that thought is true. What it consists in is, it seems to me, the thought that some deliberate action of one of them could have been the *origin* of the quarrel, the central event whose nature will by itself explain most of what happened. For it does not take much reflection to see that this just cannot be the case. Any action that either could perform could only have its effect against a background of attitudes and dispositions – facts about their relationship rather than about individual actions – and inasmuch as anything either of them could be said to have *done* is at the root of the quarrel it surely consists in gestures, tones of voice, manners of behaviour, rather than in any deliberate action.

(a) is not unusual. Most social histories have as their central causes not individual deliberate actions but complexes of attitudes and styles given which deliberate actions are just incidental precipitating factors. Social histories are caused by social situations. I take it that this is part of what family therapists mean when they urge us to avoid the idea of linear causation. But if that is so then we have a sort of paradox. For part of the picture that is to be kept at arm's length is now something central to the concept of agency: the idea that deliberate actions of human agents are a large part of the explanation of what happens to them. One of the things that family therapy suggests to us – I venture – is that this idea is just false. It is part of what bogs people down in their situations and their pointless moralising. Yet it is central to the conception of an autonomous agent. And this conception is not just of moral importance, it is also one of the things that a liberating psychotherapy aims at restoring to people: it aims at enabling people to think of themselves as deliberating agents in control of their destiny (see Lindley's and Collier's chapters in this volume). I do not want to suggest that this idea should be abandoned, but I do want to raise the suspicion that it can do with some close examination and some detailed revision.

3
FOR THE GOOD OF THE FAMILY

John Carpenter

Introduction

A postgraduate University student described her concern about her family. She had left home a few years before but would occasionally go back to see her mother and meet up with her younger sister and brother. Her brother was about to leave home and go to university; her sister was in the final year of her degree course. Their father had died some years previously. The student's concern was focussed on her sister.

The sister had been doing quite well on her course but, in the past few months, had got into a terrible state about her assessment which was of the continuous type. In order to finish every essay she would have to return home to her mother's house where she would write into the early hours in an increasingly desperate attempt to meet the deadline. Her mother would, with immense patience, minister to her needs, bringing her food, cups of coffee and ensuring that she was warm.

It was during this time that the brother left home, leaving their mother on her own, possibly for the first time in her life. Except of course that the younger sister would come home every week or so to slave over her essay and for her mother to minister to her. Furthermore, the student remarked she couldn't help but notice that the more difficult life became for her sister, the more their mother seemed to be on top of things.

In considering this example, it seems not unreasonable to observe that the effect of the sister's difficulties – whatever their cause – was to ease their mother through a difficult time, a time of transition and the loss of her last child from home. In addition, the sister's problems had been helpful to the other two children; they enabled the brother to leave home almost unnoticed and the

43

elder sister to continue living an apparently independent and relatively unconcerned life many miles away. Such analysis might well be made by a family therapist who would assume that the family's familiar coping patterns had broken down and that the symptom – the daughter's difficulties – had developed as a way of establishing a new pattern. Thus, rather than seeing the cause of the difficulties in the daughter's inadequacies, the mother's overprotectiveness or the other children's withdrawal from the family, a family therapist focusses on the change in the pattern of behaviour. The symptom is part of the new pattern in the same way as the behaviours of the other members, including mother's caring and the children's withdrawal, are also a part.

Of course, in the cases which come to the attention of a therapist, the pattern includes a symptom or behaviour which is unacceptable to them and/or to society. The request made to the therapist is to extinguish, or at least change, the symptom. However, if one part of the pattern changes, the whole pattern changes. If the difficulties are to disappear, there will be consequences for the rest of the family. In the foregoing example, the mother might become lonely and lost without a role to fulfil. She might in turn develop problems which in time could involve the other members. For this reason, Papp sees change as being not a single solution to a single problem but rather a dilemma to be resolved. 'Change extracts a price and raises the question as to what the repercussions will be for the rest of the system. To ignore these repercussions is to act out of ... ecological ignorance' (1983, p. 11).

Therefore, although it is usually individuals who are referred to them, family therapists typically assume that their 'client' is the family as a whole. An individual's symptoms, problems or difficulties are seen as evidence of a family system in difficulty, a system that is not adapting to stress from within the family or from external pressures. The solution to these problems lies not in simply curing the individual's problem because this might create worse problems for other members of the family – the solution lies in finding a new pattern of behaviour with the most positive outcome for all. Kingston, in this volume, discusses some of the ethical problems which result from family therapists' tendencies to over-focus on the family as the source and the solution of problems. In this paper, however, I will be considering the relationships between the family and its individual members.

Thus, family therapists consider as a professional ethic that they should act in order to promote the good of the family as a whole, and not necessarily in the primary interests of the individual who is referred. It is worth underlining here that it is to take up a *moral* position. There is, after all, no requirement that therapists treat all family members equally. In practice, they might insist that all members of the family attend for therapy and withhold treatment if they do not. They might allow a family member to remain distressed rather than attempting to rescue them, so that the other members, rather than the therapist, accept responsibility for dealing with the problem. They might use techniques which intensify the effects of the symptom or 'unbalance' the family system by taking sides, supporting one member and attacking another. Such actions would be justified on the grounds that, in the long term at least, the best interests of the family are in the best interests of the individual and vice versa. On the other hand, the rights of the individual to privacy and self-determination, for example, their right to choose not to attend sessions, might appear to be violated.

In this paper I would like to raise some questions concerning the extent to which an individual can be considered to have responsibilities and rights in the context of their memership of a family. I will then ask about some of the methods employed by family therapists for the good of the family as a whole.

Responsibility and cause

The postgraduate student in the example cited above was not only concerned about her family, she also described herself as feeling 'responsible'. There are apparently two senses in which she might consider herself responsible: she might believe herself causally responsible and/or she might feel a moral duty to her family. She could be responsible *for* what has happened and responsible *to* her family to put things right – whether she was responsible for it or not.

Considering causal responsibility first: a person can be responsible for something in the sense that she causes it to happen (or not to happen). Unfortunately, even when analysing the events on a billiard table, causality is never so simple and this is especially so in analysing families.

The assumption that we make is that events have causes. Thus, in a simple case, a child knocks a vase of flowers off a table. Whether the child is blamed or excused depends in large part on an analysis of preceding events, designed to establish if the act was intentional or accidental. If he had just been reprimanded for throwing his food on the floor, then the assumption would probably be that it was an intentional act displaying anger. On the other hand, if he had been reaching for the ketchup or had been bumped into by his sister, he would probably not have intended the outcome, and so not be held responsible. In the latter instance it might be his sister who was blamed. The child, who was a causal factor in the event, is in both cases responsible for what happened. The crucial element would seem to be whether or not the act was intentional and therefore whether or not the child is blameworthy. However, life is rarely so straightforward. An observer, or more likely another family member, might point out that whilst the child had indeed thrown his food on the floor, this was because his parent had been trying to force him to eat something he did not like. The parent was, therefore, also responsible for what happened. But so too was the other parent who had spent all the household money on alcohol rather than tasty food, and so on and so forth.

The search for chains of causality and intention remains, in spite of this difficulty, one of the most familiar activities in families – particularly when there has been some unfortunate or undesirable event and the search is in the interests of apportioning blame.

Thus, in the example, is the mother causally responsible for her younger daughter's difficulties? If she didn't feel lonely there would appear to be no need for the daughter to have problems. Alternatively, are the other children responsible? They left their sister to deal with their mother. Such questions seem impossible to answer in their simple form. In themselves they do not appear to represent 'sufficient' conditions or to provide the whole explanation.

Family therapists like to side-step this kind of debate, but I think it important to recognise that most family members in therapy adopt this kind of simple idea about causality. After all, they have only come to see the therapist because of the distressing or unmanageable behaviour of one of the family members. In most cases they take the view that everything would be all right, if only Mum wasn't so depressed, or Johnny stopped stealing. It is possible, of course, that these are only superficial views portrayed for the benefit of outsiders. If you were to scratch the surface you might discover more sophisticated beliefs; they might, for example, say that mother's depression is caused by her husband's intransigence on the issue of whether they should have another child, or that Johnny's stealing is a way of getting his absent mother's attention (she has left home to go and live with someone else). Nevertheless, I would maintain that simple A causes B causes C explanations and attributions of responsibility are at the heart of the beliefs of the great majority of family members whom I have seen in therapy. This has been called the 'attribution error': everyone who thinks carefully realises that you cannot attribute blame to one person alone – but most of us prefer to hold very simple views. It is tempting to attribute responsibility to ourselves when things go right and to blame others when things go wrong (Gale, personal communication).

Minuchin and Fishman (1981, p. 193) suggest that one of the goals in family therapy is to '... help family members experience their belonging to an entity that is larger than the individual self'. As family therapists, they are interested in the inter-dependence of behavioural acts. They quote, as an example, the responses of a father, mother and their young psychotic daughter, who is almost mute, to a therapist's question addressed to the daughter. Both parents answered simultaneously. When asked why they had answered when he had asked their daughter, the mother replied that her daughter made her talk. The father explained that, because the girl was always silent, they spoke for her. 'They make me silent,' contributed the girl.

Like blind men disagreeing about the shape of an elephant, Minuchin and Fishman continue, each member of the family has his or her own version of the same reality. Furthermore, most observers (or at least those brought up in Western culture) would tend to see either the girl's silence as moving her parents to answer, or the parent's quick responses as silencing their daughter. Minuchin and Fishman claim that this tendency is built into our observations, our thinking, and a language based on 'sequential grammar' (p. 194). It is extraordinarily difficult to describe simply these complementary behaviours of the family members without lapsing into the implication that one caused the other. Again, in support of the contention that most observers do indeed see in this way, I would point out that even such sophisticated students of family interaction as R. D. Laing and Aeron Esterson described the family relationships of schizophrenic girls in such a way as to make it clear that they saw the parents' attitudes and behaviour as *causing* their daughters' madness. For example, in analysing one of their cases they assert:

> We wish to emphasise here not so much the mother's evident *intra*-personal defences but that she has to defend herself from the evocation in her of her own feelings by acting on Clair (her daughter) to muddle *her* up, to render *her* speechless, to obliterate *her* memory – in short, by inducing a disorganisation *in her daughter's* personality (Laing and Esterson, 1970, p. 95).

Family therapists, on the other hand, assume that causality is complex in family interaction: it is not based on straightfoward cause and effect but rather on series of inter-connected, often simultaneous, events which link up in such a way that it becomes impossible to discern a beginning or an end. It therefore makes little sense to try and unravel who began a long-running dispute within a family and, in any case, family therapists would insist that the answer would be irrelevant to their purposes.

What family therapists assume, however, is that *every* member of the family is in some measure causally responsible for everything. So, in our example, sisters, brother and mother, perhaps other relatives, and maybe even the dead father, are responsible in part for how the family is. Some family therapists talk not of families with a psychosomatically ill or schizophrenic member but rather of psychosomatic families or of families in schizophrenic transaction. It is, to borrow the title of an early textbook on the subject, the family rather than the individual which is the 'patient' (Richter, 1974).

The therapist's goal is to help the members experience their belonging to the larger entity of the family and this is achieved by challenging their assumptions in three important respects (Minuchin and Fishman, 1981, p.194). The therapist challenges first, the family's certainty that there is one 'identified patient'; second, the 'linear' notion that this family member is controlling the others by his or her behaviour (madness, violence, etc.) and causing particular undesirable events; third, the limited, blind man's view of the elephant, replacing it with an expanded time frame which teaches family members to see their behaviour as part of a larger whole.

An individual can never claim *not* to be a member of his or her family. Leaving home might introduce an emotional as well as geographical distance into the relationship, but not breakdown. Because of the impact of this behaviour on the family, because of their common history, an individual remains a member, even as a 'ghost', whether they like it or not. Furthermore, his or her behaviour will be understood by the therapist in terms of the family as a whole.

For instance, let us suppose that the younger sister in my example had been referred to a family therapist. The therapist would very likely have attempted to convene a family meeting, including, of course, the family members who had left home. Even if the 'uninvolved' elder sister had in fact protested that it was nothing to do with her, the therapist would probably try very hard to get her to come, perceiving her distance from her mother and sister as the other side of the coin to the younger daughter's closeness to her mother. Indeed some family therapists would, if the 'uninvolved' member refused to attend for family therapy, hold the family responsible. The individual member would merely be expressing the 'resistance' felt by other members of the family in the same way that another member's schizophrenic symptoms – hearing the voices or whatever – 'say' something for the family. This notion derives from group-analytic psychology. Individuals are seen as projecting undesirable or ambivalent parts of themselves on to other members of a group who are then characterised as possessing certain qualities or behaviours, e.g. scapegoat, troublemaker. These members are then seen as expressing such behaviour on behalf of the group (see Anderson and Stewart, 1983).

From this point of view, it seems logical to make demands of the family as a whole. In order to resolve the dilemmas of change in the best interests of all its members, everyone must be involved. Effective therapy is most likely if they all attend. Non-attendance of a family member is indicative of the family's resistance to change. If therapy is going to work, the therapist must win what has been called the 'battle for structure' (Whitaker, in Haley and Hoffman 1967, p. 226). In this instance a case of one in all in – one out, all out.

I should, however, qualify these remarks by noting that in practice not all family therapists insist that everyone comes to family therapy sessions. It is not always practically possible and sometimes the therapist will decide to work with those who are motivated, whether or not other members refuse. Nevertheless, everyone who claims to be a family therapist tries to understand behaviour in terms of interactions *between people* rather than *within individuals*. Further, what family therapists do is aimed at the 'family as a system', the interventions they make in therapy are intended to influence the family as a whole.

Indeed, there are many instances in which it is preferable to work with different members of the family at different times. For example, in helping an adolescent and her parents to separate it is always profitable to have sessions with her alone if only to emphasise her developing independence. Again, some 'brief' therapists (who, whilst employing some of the same theoretical bases, have dropped any claim to be family therapists), prefer to work with the 'customer' alone (Fisch *et al.*, 1983). The customer is defined as the member of a system who wants change. This may be the wife of an alcoholic or the father of a rebellious adolescent. The goal of therapy as agreed between the customer and the brief therapist is usually to change the behaviour of the other person, the husband or the adolescent, who may neither attend, nor even be aware of, the therapy sessions.

This obviously raises the questions about the nature of the agreed goal (e.g. does it constitute an unjustifiable restriction on another's freedom, to drink or to have friends of whom your parents disapprove?). It might also raise questions about the apparent coalition between customer and therapist against other family members. However, in this case the customer soon discovers, as the therapist has known all along, that the only person's behaviour you can effectively change is your own. It is by changing your own behaviour that you create the conditions in which others might change theirs. I think this issue is essentially no different from that in so-called 'individual' therapy, much of the content of which focusses on changing the client's own feelings, attitudes and behaviour in relation to others (Dryden, 1984). If there is a difference, it lies in the family (or brief) therapist's systematic consideration of the part played by all the family members in the genesis, the continuation *and* the solution to the (family) problem. Whether you attend the session with the rest of your family or not, it is impossible to escape the attentions of a family therapist.

I have already suggested that most members of families seen in therapy perceive the situation rather differently from their therapist. Because they have a different understanding of causality it seems to me that family therapy almost inevitably involves a deception of the family members by the therapist. I think they are deceived by the therapist as to what will be required of them. This deception, which is not in my opinion dependent on the style or method of family therapy employed, arises because therapists on the whole believe that family members would be unlikely to engage in therapy if the therapist's view of their joint (causal) responsibility were to be spelt out at the very beginning. Tactically it is much better for such a realisation to emerge gradually, and by then, of course, the family members have been 'hooked in'. Nevertheless, the discovery that even the most uninvolved members will have to change their behaviour is often a profound event, and it is quite possible that they would not have agreed to take part in the therapy sessions if they had known this at the beginning. I will return to this issue of the consequences of family therapy unforeseen by the family members later.

Responsibility, rights and duties

The student of my example described a sense of responsibility to her family – a responsibility to put things right. She felt that she had a moral duty to help with her sister's difficulties. This duty would be based on an implicit contract with the other members of her family to the effect that they should rally round when one is in trouble. In a similar situation another person might have denied any such responsibility. He or she might have been more concerned with their 'rights' as an individual, including their right to privacy. In an extreme form they might argue their right not to be a member of a family and therefore not to attend therapy or indeed have anything to do with the family. Such an argument is not uncommon, at least in Western societies.

On the other hand, I suspect that family therapy would be a good deal easier to practise in less aggressively individualistic cultures. For as Clayre (1984) observes of China:

> Religion and philosophy in China have put family first and community a close second, ahead of any such aims in life as individual happiness or freedom. The state has added its influence on the same side, supporting the family with its laws ... The Chinese live in a tight mesh of relationships and obligations in which each person is both supported and under surveillance ... (1984, pp. 92–3).

Clayre describes the case of a young couple referred to a 'mediation committee' in which the wife had sued for divorce. This followed her husband's attempt to have her sewn up during a Caesarian section in order to suffocate his own child, which he had discovered was a girl rather than a boy. The mediation was a lengthy process, involving not only the couple themselves but also both extended families and even representatives of the couple's respective work-units. As Clayre comments, there was '... a feeling perhaps on the part of both husband and wife, that no solution was likely to be accepted by the committee as a final outcome except a reconciliation between them'. Eventually this was what they agreed, and they were shown two years later apparently reasonably happy as individuals.

Like Chinese mediators, then, family therapists focus on the family rather than on its individual members. Do they share similar assumptions about families? I suspect not, but this does prompt me to ask about the kinds of model families therapists have in, or just out of, mind.

'Good' families

Before asking what is a 'good' or model family, we should first ask what is a family. For, though I think it very unlikely that there are any family therapists naive enough to define a family as husband and wife plus 2.4 children, there may be some rather woolly assumptions abroad. In fact, a recent review of family therapy literature by the sociologist D. H. J. Morgan concluded that whilst the conventional nuclear family household is assumed to be the model, answers to the pragmatic question of whom to include in family sessions reflected wider theoretical assumptions about the nature of the family. He expressed surprise that: '... contrary to my expectations, the family therapists were aware of variations in the definition and understanding of the family' (Morgan, 1985, p. 46).

Most family therapists decline to provide a definition of the family in their writings and, with the notable exception of Minuchin (1974), do not provide a clear account of their model of a good family. This has not, however, prevented feminist critics from exposing the often blatant sexist assumptions inherent in much of the literature (e.g. Hare-Mustin, 1978; Osborne, 1983; Golder, 1985). Golder, for example, asserts that family therapists '... have taken a snapshot of white middle-class family life in the '50s and mistaken it for a Platonic model of family structure'. She argues that the women's role as the guardian of the family developed as part of a social and economic process. The over-involved mother and peripheral father of the archetypal 'family case' should be seen in their historical context, rather than being taken as evidence of family 'pathology'. Golder suggests that most family therapists convey confusing messages to 'over-involved' mothers, asking them on the one hand to 'step aside' and on the other requiring them to ensure that the family stays in therapy. 'In other words, we utilise the very centrality we challenge, we rely on the very traits of character we critique, and in essence, without realising it, we exploit women's helpless social position, all in the service of gaining therapeutic leverage.' Thus, an assumption about the respective roles of women and men in parenting – that they should both be involved – leads to women's further oppression.

It is certainly questionable to assume that the interests of individual family members coincide either with each other or with the interests of the family as a whole – whatever they are and whosoever defines them. Minuchin, for example, characterises the process of socialisation of the child as 'inherently conflictual'. He points out that parents cannot protect and guide their children without at the same time controlling them and restricting their activities. Similarly, children cannot develop emotionally and become individuated without rejecting and attacking their parents (Minuchin, 1974, p. 58). Most dramatically this occurs during adolescence, but it is an element in all stages of a child's psychological development. Such conflict is grist to the therapist's mill, and its outcome, which will not necessarily favour all equally, cannot be independent of the therapist's own influence. If the therapist were able not to influence the outcome, then the interests of the most powerful member would probably win out. The discussion of power in families is one which has caused much disagreement among family therapists. Bateson (1973, p. 462), for example, claims that its use in relationships is 'a myth' and he goes on to suggest that '... some current thinking about family systems leads to a belief that the rules which underpin relationship patterns are formed by a consensus of family members'. Kingston (1982) effectively demolishes this claim, proposing firstly that we ask the 'dangerous' question, 'Who benefits most from a particular rule?' and then consider the situation where a couple with children separate. He points out that one or both adults take the decision – the children do not.

So where does that leave the therapist? If the therapist chooses to take sides, how does she make her choice? If you are a family therapist it is by no means clear who is your client. It would be misleading to claim that the family is your client. The family cannot speak. Its members say different things. In practice, I for one, and I suspect I am not alone, fall back on certain culturally derived assumptions about how families should be, which include, amongst others, assumptions about the rights of individual members of families at different ages. (Watson, in Chapter 1 of this volume, argues that these assumptions include those which lie behind systems theory and behind Bowlby's theory of attachment behaviour, both of which are ultimately derived from biology.)

I do try to listen carefully in order to ascertain what the individual members want for themselves. This in itself is often a challenge. Many women have great difficulty in answering questions about their *own* needs – they have not assumed that these are of any importance and frequently cannot even articulate them. On the other hand, one individual might demand something which I consider inappropriate, for example, a man, to his wife's evident distress, demands his 'right' to keep a mistress. Here, my own values rise to the surface and I deliberately try to influence the more powerful to respect the need or wishes of the less powerful.

In the case of families with children (minors in the legal sense) I often resort to claiming the position of 'expert'. There is a body of knowledge in developmental psychology from which I feel reasonably confident in making assertions about the developmental needs of children. With respect to adults, the same knowledge does not exist and I hesitate to make similar pronouncements. Nevertheless, I do on occasion tell people what they *ought* to do – not always in such a straightforward manner – and here my intention is to influence them.

I should make it clear that I deliberately try not to influence a position or a goal which does seem to have been agreed on by all parties. For example, if a husband and wife state that they want a less intimate, more business-like marriage, then I would not consider it my task to persuade them of the joys of a close relationship. However, if their goals are such that I consider them morally wrong, then I would decline to work with them. If they were both morally and legally wrong it would be my duty to inform them of this fact and to decline to work with them.

My job would certainly be easier if I could be sure that all my clients shared my assumptions, as they might in China, and even if they did not, I might think that I knew what was best or right for them.

Consequences of therapy

One of the difficulties of being a family therapist is that you cannot claim ignorance of the consequences of your therapy. As an individual therapist I could be quite uninterested in the effects on a husband of my efforts to help his wife, my client, to 'grow' and to express her individuality. However, family therapists are not in the business of simply minimising unhappiness; indeed in the short term at least, we frequently allow or even promote distress in individual family members.

Of course, distress in therapy is nothing new – confronting painful issues from the past or challenging truths about themselves is an inevitable consequence of individual therapy. What is different in family therapy however, is that the members who experience the distress are not only or necessarily the members who have come identified as 'clients'.

Thus, as a family therapist I will try to make the members of a family accept responsibility for dealing with a difficult member. I will not simply and easily accede to a request that this member be admitted to a mental hospital or received into care. If that member does go, I will ensure that the decision is theirs and not mine. They will not like it and will probably become quite distressed, but in the long term I believe that this will make the problem less likely to recur.

This issue is also exemplified in the techniques which some family therapists use. I will consider briefly two common examples. The first is that of escalating the problem or symptom: the parents of a quiet, good-tempered 14-year-old girl bring her to a therapist because she has anorexia nervosa. She eats virtually nothing, is rapidly losing weight, and will soon be admitted to hospital. Her parents are very concerned and anxious that their daughter's illness is treated. The therapist says that, if they do not want her taken into hospital, *they* must *make* her eat at home. The daughter refuses angrily, shouting insults at her mother and father who are distressed but, following the therapist's instructions, they increase their demands. The girl becomes even more angry and insulting. The immediate effect of the parents' compliance is to stress all three family members most severely. The therapist's intention is to make them see each other in a different light, in particular for the parents to perceive their child as disobedient, stubborn and strong rather than ill, helpless and weak. In this way they might move from being over-protective and over-controlling to demanding that their daughter become responsible for herself and her own body (and allowing her to do so).

Similarly, the therapist might try to 'unbalance' the family system by ceasing to be 'fair', taking sides, and supporting one member whilst attacking another. A husband, his son and prospective daughter-in-law come to family meetings at the therapist's request in order to help his mentally ill wife. This woman behaves childishly, acts irresponsibly and talks nonsense in the session. To the whole family's surprise, the therapist praises her great sensitivity and understanding of her family's needs and acknowledges the sacrifice she is making on their behalf. He attacks the son and his girlfriend (implying that their relationship is uncertain) and says that they are using his mother's illness as an excuse for not getting married. In the same way he attacks the husband, saying that he would find it too threatening to have a capable wife. The intention, and the effect, in this case was for the wife to give up her crazy behaviour and for the rest of the family to prove the therapist mistaken: the husband ceased to undermine his wife and the son left home and married his girlfriend.

These various activities, insisting that all attend, making them accept responsibility, stressing individual family members, all rest on the assumption that an individual's symptoms or problematic behaviour are evidence of a family in trouble. But, family therapists employ a theoretical model of causality which is different from those commonly used and accepted by their clients. Since this model is used to justify the actions of therapists which, at first sight, run counter to the wishes of individuals, the validity of the model itself should be open for examination. To what extent is the systems model an accurate representation of real life?

The systems model of the family has been criticised, as it is in this volume by

Kingston, for the lack of attention given to systems which impinge on the family from outside, by Watson for its abandonment of ideas of moral agency and its reductionist view of human beings in relationship, and by Morton for its loss of a theory of causality which preserves the autonomy of the individual. There have been but two substantial studies of normal family functioning from the systems perspective, and both of these are of white, middle-class families in the United States (Lewis *et al.*, 1976; Kantor and Lehr, 1973). Whilst both studies seem to demonstrate that the systems model can provide a good description of these families, its wider applicability remains questionable.

Secondly, what are the consequences of believing this model to be an accurate representation of reality? The issues involved seem to be both conceptual and moral. They appear to include: the reification of the 'family system'; issues of causation and the responsibility of individuals for the workings of a system; and the rights of individuals in the context of their membership of a family group.

I conclude with a typical dilemma. The husband of a severely depressed woman referred to a family therapy clinic said to me: I don't mind coming along – so long as I don't get too involved. How do I judge how much to involve him? How much distress can I cause him in the interests of his wife's mental health and/or their marital relationship? After all, if she does stop being depressed then their marriage might end in divorce. Which would be preferable and for whom?

4

IN PRAISE OF FEELING: THEME-FOCUSSED FAMILY WORK

Una McCluskey

Introduction

The importance of acknowledging people's feelings as an integral part of their sense of self and identity has a long tradition in the history of the caring professions. Philosophers and theologians, such as Binswanger (1963), Buber (1923), MacMurray (1932, 1957, 1961) and Dunstan (1982), psychiatrists, such as Rogers (1961, 1969) and Frankl (1973), social workers, such as Hollis (1964) and Ford (1979 and 1983), and family therapists, such as Satir (1967, 1976), Bowen (1972), Whitaker (1975 and 1982), Boszormenyi-Nagy (1965 and 1973), Lieberman (1979), and Byng-Hall (1973) have all in their separate and sometimes quite different ways asserted the power of feeling as a source of energy, creativity, irrationality, connectedness and meaning, in human relationships. With the exception of Satir and Whitaker, these other practitioners have seen feeling as only one important element amongst others that they attend to in their work with families. In the model which I describe feelings become the central thematic focus of the work with the family. The worker helps the family to concentrate on the experience of being in their families.

The approach emphasises that people in a family need space, time and opportunity to explore for themselves the meaning of their *feelings* in response to their experience of being in their family, and to discover the meaning in their *behaviour* and that of others in the light of this. It is my belief that a person's confidence is shattered, and their sense of self eroded, when their feeling experience within the family is constantly denied, overruled or misinterpreted. Theme-focussed work highlights this process when it occurs. It tries to counteract it by taking seriously what people say so that they get a sense of being responded to and of making a meaningful impact on others. In my view this facilitates the development of an integrated sense of self. This approach assists individuals in separating themselves out from each other in a way that helps them to unravel what belongs to them and what is put on to them or into them from outside. My intentions in this paper are to describe this way of working, with particular reference to the role of the worker; to examine the beliefs and assumptions underlying it, as well as the ethical principles and issues arising from it, and finally, to look at the management of these ethical issues in practice.

Theme-focussed family work

Theme-focussed family therapy is fundamentally about working with the feelings, emotional and physical, which family members are experiencing in response to some crisis or event. Thus a family who was experiencing a divorce or removal of a child or children into care might be offered sessions on the theme comings and goings in this family and what people feel about them. The method is called *theme-focussed* because the primary task of each session is to work on the theme. The worker's job is to make sure that everyone is listened to, their contributions attended to, and the meaning of these contributions explored in relation to the theme. The worker assumes that individual contributions are related to the theme, even when the connection is not obvious. It then becomes the task of the family group to work at what the connection might be. Sticking to the task in this fashion, however bizarre it might appear in any particular instance, does create an ethos within the group that contributions are meaningful and relevant.

Criteria for undertaking theme-focussed work

The worker should have some evidence that the individuals have a sense of belonging to the same family and a capacity to care about each other. Furthermore, the family members should express a wish to be seen as a group in order to understand better and possibly resolve some of their problems.

The choice of theme and how it is framed

The choice of theme is obviously critical to the nature of the work that gets done. The worker must identify issues which individuals in the family have had to face or are facing, and also issues which are being faced by the whole family. For example, the whole family might have moved house recently and individuals within the family might also have faced particular crises that have a transitional nature to them (not specifically connected with the house move). By looking at the family as a whole, as well as at individuals within it, the worker can build up some ideas for a theme that will capture the connection between them all as well as hold on to their individuality. The worker should check her own feelings and responses to working with the family as a whole, because these might give her a further clue as to what the family is finding most difficult. Once a theme is beginning to form in the worker's mind she should check it over to see whether it would have meaning for everyone in the family.

The work is about unravelling complex emotions and behaviours. Any theme chosen to promote this process must include the following features:

(i)   it must be a simple statement so that it can be held in consciousness by all the family members;
(ii) it needs to be framed at a sufficiently general level that the individuals can use it in their own way and for their own purposes;
(iii) it needs to be sufficiently particular that it captures an issue that is of relevance to all the family members.

Thus one might construct a theme as 'loss in this family and how people feel about it' rather than 'Granny's death and how people feel about it'. The former allows for many more possibilities and dimensions to be explored than does the latter.

The role of the worker in theme-focused work

The worker should ensure the following:

(i)   that the family keep to the purpose of the session, and that means, inter alia, pursuing the chosen theme;
(ii) that everyone is heard;
(iii) that individuals pay attention to each other's non-verbal cues, particularly when these are signalling distress; and

(iv) that they check out their perceptions and understanding of each other with each other.

Keeping individuals purposive in this way of working is a task that is shared by worker and family. A particular feature of this approach is that it deals with hierarchical relationships and the attendant power structure in those relationships in a different way to either the structural or strategic schools of family therapy. Children are given the same status as adults, in that they have authority for defining how they feel. This work is not about how the family is *functioning*, it is about how the individuals in the family are *feeling*. The need for changes in family structure and functioning might become apparent to the family as the work progresses, but in the first instance the work is about enabling family members to hear what their experience is of each other. It is left with the family to decide whether they want help with changing their structure and functioning in response to a deeper knowledge and understanding of each other. In this work it is vital that *all* family members are encouraged to communicate what they are feeling because how each individual manages his or her feelings affects everyone – contributions from parents and children are taken equally seriously.

The worker may need to help the family revise assumptions they may hold about each other's capacity to feel. Everybody, whatever their age or status or role position, is asked to abide by the following rule. Nobody is sanctioned to invade the boundaries of another and declare on their behalf what they are thinking or feeling. When everyone accords each other this level of respect, then there is space and time for all family members to help each other articulate their experience in a way that feels accurate to them and meaningful to everyone.

People's feelings about themselves and others will always be a complicated mixture of what they have taken in from society through membership of its various organisations and institutions, and their experience in the family now. The work must be kept open, the meaning of experiences and events must be fully explored and not restricted to individual prejudices or worker's theories.

To facilitate this work the worker needs to pay attention to what is being said and to attend to the sequence of the discussion while keeping the theme in mind. The worker might ask the family to pay attention to how their contributions follow one from the other. This process can often help the family members to listen more attentively to what each one is saying, to attend to free associations and to become aware of the richness of the connection between individual contributions. It is surprising how connected apparently disparate contributions become when they are placed in the context of the theme. It is very quickly obvious to the family how inter-connected as people they all are: so connected that they can sometimes do things for one another out of unconscious identification, rather than conscious choice. Although it must be obvious to the reader that the thrust of this work is to facilitate the individuation of family members, one of its inevitable consequences is to affirm the connections between them, even if at the end of the day they decide it is not in their interests to remain living together. I have had children say to parents in the course of this work that they want to remain in contact with their parents but wish to *live* elsewhere.

Dealing with conflict

The process of the work itself is inevitably stressful. Parents and children do not always want or need the same thing, and may, therefore, be in conflict with each other. An example of this is a family in which the parents have decided on separation or divorce, but the children or child is very against losing their father or mother from the household. The work demands that the worker get close to the experiences of the family and sometimes this can be quite distressing. Very often what family members are saying to each other is something which they and the worker might prefer not to hear. It means the worker has to sit and listen to what individual members have to say about how they feel about being in the family. The worker may want to curtail or not attend to something a family member is saying in order to protect either herself or other family members from hearing it. The worker should not forget that the family, including the youngest member, is living with whatever 'it' is, and talking about it may be worse than the experience itself. However, if it is being talked about in the presence of the worker, the worker can make sure that those most affected have the chance to respond and make their feelings and reactions known and understood. Such work nearly always involves the worker in clarifying roles and responsibilities with family members, so that individuals are clear what it is they are taking responsibility for. For example, a child who makes clear his views that the family should not move house should not afterwards be held accountable if the house burns down. While this way of working encourages individuals to state what they want and need (in much the same way as Satir talks about in her book *Peoplemaking*, 1976), it must be made clear amongst family members how responsibility is being shared and carried when decisions are made.

The worker may seek to stop the process of exploring feelings (i.e. individual reactions and experiences) for many reasons. Perhaps whatever is being discussed resonates too deeply with some experience inside herself. Perhaps the worker is suspicious about the expression of feeling, knowing that feelings can lead to action and actions can be destructive. In this context it is necessary again to examine what is meant by 'expressing' feelings and the connection between feeling and action. I do not intend to convey that telling people what you feel about them is necessarily a good thing, or for that matter a destructive thing. It can be used to make someone feel good or feel bad, which is essentially using feelings to create an effect in someone else. It can also be used as a first step in unravelling what one's true feeling for another is. For example, a mother might say to her son that she does not love him and that she never has done. This mother might be expressing something she believes and in words she thinks appropriate, and may not be saying this as a way of hurting her son. The worker would be failing in her task if she left things there, and didn't explore with the mother the meaning of the remark, and its impact on the son and other members of the family with them. Having rules about what one's experience of another ought to be can prevent one from naming and seeking to understand one's actual experience. For example, if one has a rule for oneself that says one should not feel hate for another person, then that rule can get in the way of knowing one's experience of another directly inside oneself and making sense of it. If one can accept one's feeling, one can go on and look at what it makes one want to do and the possible consequences and effects of that. In this way feelings and behaviour do become more meaningfully linked. For instance, in the example above, the mother may go on to say that perhaps it is not that she does not love her son, but that it would be more accurate to say that she does not experience the same feeling inside herself that she recognises she feels for someone else. Whatever the next stage of clarification is, it can be pursued in such a way that all the individuals in the family are encouraged to communicate what they are saying, how they are affected by what they hear, and what action it makes them want to take. Saying that one's feelings for one person are different from those for another at least opens the discussion to include the possibility that one is as much making statements about oneself as defining, condemning, or applauding the object of those feelings. The family's difficulties are not going to be resolved by sitting on the expression of feeling. In fact, if the worker stops an exploration of the meaning of the feelings that are being expressed this can prevent both worker and family from hearing clearly what is going on and what action if any needs to be taken.

Non-verbal communication

In this kind of work it is vital that the worker pays attention to the non-verbal cues of the family members. She must note the reactions of individuals to what is being said and take the time to get in touch herself with her own physical and emotional reactions to what is happening. Very often one gets clues about what is going on inside someone from a change in their tone of voice, facial expression, or bodily position. There may even be less obvious physical signs, such as a change in the noise level in the room, as when one experiences a very deep stillness or a burst of sudden activity. What is important to note is the change from one state to another, and to encourage the family to become more sensitised to these changes in themselves and each other so that they can become more deeply aware of how and what they communicate. At any stage in a discussion on a theme, what a person is saying might appear innocuous or insignificant up to such a point, but then it becomes obvious to those present that it has a power and a depth to it which as yet has not been put into words. The point at which a person begins to put into words experiences and emotions which have remained until that moment silent within can appear very risky, and be very frightening for the person and those present in the room. If the worker can allow herself to get emotionally involved in what is happening as well as remaining supremely attentive to the detail of it and the context in which it is happening, she can support herself and the other in bringing forth whatever it is that needs to be communicated and to be heard. Being attentive to non-verbal responses and developing the skills necessary to put into words what is happening is something that in my experience the family learn very quickly to do for themselves. There is a power to this work, and a depth and a richness to it, which has a healing quality, and this is invigorating and refreshing in spite of the tension and strain that can accompany it.

Making the environment a safe place

The worker obviously needs help to keep the work going – and to keep it related to the task. This kind of work can only be productive in a safe environment: that is, an environment where people can feel they are being heard and where attempts will be made to make sense of what they are saying. A worker should be aware when it is that she stops what is being said or changes the subject, because this may be an indication that she is begining to feel unsafe. If the worker is feeling unsafe then she is not going to be able to provide the 'mental holding' necessary for the family to explore safely what it is they are saying to one another. This kind of holding has been beautifully described by Winnicott (1941, 1957, 1960) in his reference to the work of the 'good enough mother' who responds to the child's exploration of reality in a way that facilitates rather than impinges on this process, and which allows the child to develop a true self capable of coming to terms with the realities which are both internal and external to the self. The worker may need help from her supervisor or family therapy team if she is feeling unsafe with the family, in order to sort out whether her uneasiness is coming from herself or the family. In this kind of work a worker cannot predict what is going to happen, she can only commit herself to stay with it and see it through.

To keep the work going the worker must be assured of effective supervision/consultation and organisational support. This level of involvement with a family can be very frightening for a worker. Real fears are touched in the family which have to be held on to and explored. These fears can sometimes be too much for a worker who may feel that neither she nor the family can handle them. If she cannot get help from an outside person or support group to make sense of what is happening she risks getting stuck in a nightmare of fear with the family, thus inducing more chaos and violence than were there originally. Organisationally, workers and their supervisors or support groups need to be given adequate time and space both to do the work itself and to role-play, re-enact and think through what they are doing. The more interruptions from other work there are into the space available to do this the more unsafe the worker is in terms of being able to rely on herself to be in touch with the impact of what is happening and the meaning of it. The main assumption behind this work is that feelings can have a powerful impact on behaviour. Organisationally this must be recognised if the worker is to get the support she needs to hold on to feelings aroused in her by the family and explore their meaning.

Assumptions and beliefs underlying theme-focussed family work

Making a list of beliefs and assumptions is necessarily arbitrary. The problems with such an endeavour are that one risks leaving out some essential point, or being unnecessarily repetitive, or giving a false impression that working with feeling is logical, progressive and calm. Feeling has its own logic, but working intimately with people is confusing, taxing emotionally, and mentally exhausting, as well as having the invigorating quality that is around when people are talking about something that is real and that matters to them. Here are some observations about the role of emotions.

Everyone has emotions. Emotions are responsive to real events, either inside or outside the person. These real events are identifiable, thus making the emotion at least understandable if not more manageable. Intense emotion needs to be faced, held on to inside in order to be recognised and understood. If it is not, behaviour can appear meaningless, disconnected and unpredictable. Recognising or admitting to emotions, however awful one might feel them to be, does not mean that as a person one is only what one feels to be at that moment, e.g. empty, useless, bad, confused, damaging. People also need to learn or remember that they can choose whether or not to act on their feelings. Accepting one's emotional reactions and claiming ownership of them is the first step towards identifying behaviour that is linked to those emotions. Establishing a link between feeling and behaviour may permit an understanding of the behaviour, where it previously appeared meaningless and arbitrary. Acknowledging and taking responsibility for one's emotions is a necessary part of remaining in touch with one's continuity over time.

In troubled families it is not always clear which emotion is being experienced by whom, because the boundaries between people are blurred. People's capacity to perceive a boundary that separates what they feel from what another person feels varies according to age and maturity; in times of stress anybody's capacity can be diminished. Recognising that other people feel differently from one's self may mean the shattering of illusions. However, coming to terms with reality has its own healing process, as the work on death and bereavement has shown (Pincus, 1974; Kubler-Ross, 1975; Marris, 1974; Parkes, 1972). Dismissing a person's feelings is an assault on the fundamental identity of that person; engaging with another person's feelings is to risk assaulting one's own.

Ethical principles underlying theme-focussed work

1   All persons in the family, of whatever age, have the right to have their views heard and the reality of their emotions accepted; therefore no person has the right to dismiss what another is saying about what they are thinking or feeling.
2   The worker ought to act selectively in relating to members of the family where necessary in order to minimise distress and possible harm.
3   The worker must not coerce members of the family to work in this way.

The management of ethical issues in practice

The following are some of the features of this way of working, which raise ethical questions for practice:

1 The power of the worker

Guggenbuhl-Craig (1982) has drawn our attention to the way in which we can misuse our power in relation to clients. Workers can damage as well as help their clients. If the worker can accept that they *can* damage others through misuse of their power then they have to be constantly alert to the possibility.

It may also be suggested that we use our professional power inappropriately and possibly destructively if we name as family problems issues that have their origin and maintenance in the larger structures in society (see Kingston, chapter 9 in this volume).

The power differential between worker and family takes on another dimension when one takes into account that families are not composed of individuals who are accorded the same status by society. Family members differ in terms of age and gender, and both these factors influence to a large extent the power and authority accorded to them by their culture and the society within which they live (Gittings, 1985). They also differ by virtue of their ability or personal resources (such as independent financial means). Workers can contribute to or diminish this inequality. Power is both something that an individual has within him or her, and something conferred by society on persons who are in particular social positions by virtue of their age, sex, occupation and control over resources. These ideas are explored more fully in a paper by Haldane, McCluskey and Clark, 1986. These two aspects, the inner world of experience and the outer world of reality, influence one another. There is a tension between these two worlds; the individual is the reference point for this tension, and individuals can be encouraged to speak and act authentically from this experience. While individuals can become more conscious of their use of power and relationship to it, and go on to make some changes in their behaviour within the family through this kind of work, this should not blind us to the existence of massive inequalities in the distribution of power in the outside world which require action of a different order.

2 Responsibility of the worker in relation to choosing the theme

A worker will only select a theme after spending some time with a family in getting to know their individual preoccupations. She develops a notion for a theme from a position of being outside the family and of being in relation to all the family members and not just to one. Such a position allows the worker to frame a theme in a way that captures something essential for all the family members. It follows that this kind of work demands that the worker pay attention to the *individuals* and what they say about their experience in the family, that she also pays attention to *relationships* within the family and that *she is open* with the family about what she thinks the problems are and what she thinks might help. In identifying a theme she thinks is going to be relevant to the family dynamics, the worker is assuming the right to say that she can see something and put things together in a way she thinks the family need to work on. The ethical implications may be that the family should be given the opportunity to challenge this view and negotiate with the worker on what the theme should be, or refuse the worker's offer of this kind of help.

3 Interpreting behaviour with reference to the theme

The theme is meant to encapsulate something that connects individuals in the family to one another; for example, loss, illness or expansion in family membership. In line with other family therapy approaches, the worker shifts the attention of the family from one individual whom they may have identified as the problem to be sorted out, to things that are happening in the family that affect everyone. While structural family therapists engage with issues of power and control in the family, changing internal family alliances working with sub-systems and transactions across boundaries, an existential therapist is less prescriptive about how the family should alter their internal organisation. Theme-focussed work is based on a hypothesis concerning the key emotional issues for the family. It structures sessions around this hypothesis, thus allowing very little hiding space to the family where they could avoid coping with their emotional realities. In this way it is not unlike strategic family therapy, in that the family is manipulated into a position where they are confronted with themselves. In strategic work it is important that the worker does not share her hypothesis with the family – in theme-focussed work the opposite is true. In strategic work one anticipates how the family is likely to respond to one's interventions – in theme-focussed work one has no idea how individuals are going to pursue the theme, or what sense they are going to discover in what happens. Though the role of interpreter is encouraged by the worker to pass from her to the family, she nevertheless keeps the family to task. This she does by asking family members to show the relevance of their contribution to the theme. Thus, whatever they do or say is seen as associative to the theme unless proved otherwise, e.g. when remarks are shown to be redundant. A 13-year-old boy told his family in a session that because of a recent incident that had jogged his memory, he regarded the onset of his epilepsy as dating from the time he witnessed his father drunk and he himself had suffered physical injury as a result. He went on to establish that his adopted role of intermediary in his parents' quarrels usually precipitated an epileptic attack. (He went on to confirm his own hypothesis by having a seizure in a session while his parents were arguing.) The theme for these sessions was 'What it feels like to be a member of this family'. The important point to note is that it was the child *himself* who established meaning in his behaviour, and not the worker. Also pertinent here is that the family saw their 'problem' as the aggressive disruptive behaviour of a younger daughter. Other forms of family work may have helped to resolve the daughter's symptoms and the family functioning, but would they have allowed the son to gain this new understanding for himself?

4 Permission from the family to work in this way

This work is essentially open-ended (Haldane and McCluskey, 1982). As such it is difficult, if not impossible, to give individuals a clear idea at the begining of what they are letting themselves in for. Nor can one identify any predefined end. There is no way of knowing what experiences individuals are going to get in touch with within themselves. However, one can be clear about the process of the work and what it is likely to involve. The worker should tell the family that the purpose of the sessions is to explore their feelings in relation to the theme and that, therefore, the process of the work will involve making sense of their contributions in the light of the theme. In that sense seeking permission to work in this way is asking family members to trust the process involved in communicating what they feel about themselves and about each other. The worker uses her practice experience to assess whether this family have enough of a sense of family connectedness and commitment to each other's well-being to make this a worthwhile venture. Making such an assessment always contains an element of risk. Consent in this endeavour means consenting to an attempt to be honest in one's communication about what one is experiencing.

5 The rights of children within the family

This way of working demands considerable honesty from all concerned, and thus raises the question whether children should be protected from hearing from parents or other adult attachment figures things which distress and cause them pain. It also raises the issue of whether we think children should be protected from parental worries, expressions of distress, statements of self-doubt, anger or other displays of emotion which might be upsetting to children.

The practice implications are that one has to assess how much of this the children have been exposed to in any case, and whether or not they are likely to see or hear anything in the sessions that would be totally new to them. The worker should encourage all family members, including children, to state if and when they have heard enough from each other, and ensure that this is respected. A dilemma for the worker might arise if one member vetoes the discussion but the rest wish to continue. In this case it may be necessary for the worker to examine issues of power and responsibility openly with the family and look at the implications of different people having different roles and functions. This should provide a base for the worker from which to help the family work out how to proceed. Whatever the rights of children to have some protection from adults, children have the fundamental right to speak for themselves, and to hear the views of others so that what they say might be informed.

6 *Training and supervision; seeking permission from the worker to share their responses and reactions to the family with their supervisor*

As in the work itself, it is impossible to predict with the trainee what is likely to arise for them in the course of working with families which comes out of experiences of being in their own family. One can, however, be clear with the trainee that working with families inevitably puts one in touch with one's own family experience, and that this sometimes gets in the way of distinguishing what belongs to the family one is working with and what belongs to oneself. The processes of supervision are somewhat similar to the process of the work itself in that the supervisor will focus on the worker's emotional responses in relation to the work and seek to understand these. The worker is expected to discuss the impact the family is having on her, what sense she makes of it, and what she wants to do about it, so that this action can be examined with the supervisor with regard to whether it is in the interests of the family. The worker aims to help the family examine their feelings in relation to what is happening to them in order to increase their understanding of their own behaviour. It is important that this process is mirrored in supervision, as the worker is not immune to getting caught up in the same dynamic that the family are in. This allows the worker the opportunity to explore the impact of the family on her and to examine her feelings and behaviour in the light of the theme. She is then able to use her understanding to inform her behaviour with the family and to make this understanding available to them. The work is about holding on to emotional reactions so that they can be understood, rather than simply acted out. For example, a worker I was supervising in this way once returned from a short Christmas break to find that in her absence the mother of the family she was working with had rung the emergency services on Christmas day and had the children removed into care. As the theme that was being worked with in this family was comings and goings in the family, it seemed appropriate to handle this situation with reference to it. The worker, therefore, convened the family and initiated a discussion with them on the theme, this time introducing her own feelings about what had happened in her absence and the impact the mother's behaviour in particular had had on her. This allowed the family to come to grips with some of the bizarre nature of their behaviour which sometimes accompanied feelings of loss and abandonment, but where the underlying feelings were never acknowledged or understood between them. In this form of work the supervisor must pay attention to the theme the worker is working on so that the worker's own emotional responses can be used in the work, thus making *her own behaviour* intelligible to herself and the family. The reader should not be left with the impression that this way of working is akin to self-disclosure on the part of the worker. That is where the worker refers to their own experiences in order to make a link with the family. When the worker introduces her own material to the family it should be (a) clear that her responses are directly related to the theme; and (b) that she uses what she has to say in order to engage the family with herself to make sense of her experience. Thus she offers a model for working on emotional reactions which involves sticking with them and making sense of them, rather than simply acting them out.

As in the work described by Mattinson and Sinclair (1979), the worker may sometimes go through the process of behaving just like the family before she can see what the problem is, what is happening and what she needs to change about her own behaviour. In the example just given, the worker's initial response to finding that the children had been removed into care in her absence was to feel both angry and despairing. (This family had been worked with unsuccessfully by a series of different workers and agencies over many years – this knowledge added to the worker's despair.) What the worker needed to do was to refrain from getting caught up in her own reactions and instead take the action described. In this way supervision of the worker sometimes needs to mirror the work she is doing with the family. The worker may decide she does not want to expose herself to this kind of supervision. The dilemma arising from such an attitude is that there are very few controls on what family therapists choose to do or what kind of supervision or support they get once they have acquired the techniques of practice.

Conclusion

At the beginning of this paper I acknowledged some of the many people who have influenced my way of working and determined my interest in making feelings the central focus for work. By way of conclusion I would like to assert that the family is a social and economic unit and exists in a cultural, political and ideological context (Gittings, 1985; Kingston, chapter 9 in this volume). Belief systems prevalent in society and translated through its structures and organisations permeate the individuals' own value systems, their feelings, their sense of self. Although this way of working emphasises the emotional responses of individuals in the family, as well as taking account of the worker's emotional responses to the family, the work is about paying attention to the individual in the context she inhabits. This sometimes means challenging the assumptions, attitudes and values themselves, which have their genesis in social or political constructs.

Because the network that influences and shapes a person's values and self-worth is so intricate, it seems to me that there is every reason for starting with and staying with what the person says they are experiencing inside themselves, taking it seriously and exploring its meaning with them. Outside realities of an interpersonal, organisational or political nature must not be seen as having their source within the individual. What an individual communicates about their feelings, however, may well have to be understood and acted upon at those levels. The implication of this way of thinking and working is that as a worker one must be prepared to have one's own framework for understanding and making sense of people's experience and behaviour extended.

In this chapter I have described a form of family work which is essentially open-ended in its aims and which takes personal meaning and experience as the primary focus for attention. This work highlights the reciprocal nature of the relationship between the worker and the family, and suggests that changes in one part of the client-worker system affect changes in the other. In this kind of encounter the worker must expect to be changed as well as the family. Because the work is exploratory and focusses on experience and personal meaning one cannot predict the outcome in advance. The skills in this work become accessible to the family, especially the children whose capacity for seeing what is there to be seen, hearing what there is to be heard, and knowing what they feel, is often much greater than our own.

Theme-focussed work takes as its domain the highly personal and private area of people's lives – their feelings. The work is carried out with the intention that members of a family become clearer about the meaning of their interactions with each other and therefore can choose with more integrity what they do.

5

FEMINIST THERAPY AND FAMILY THERAPY: THE LIMITS TO THE ASSOCIATION

Sue Walrond-Skinner

The purpose of this chapter is to examine the relationship between family therapy, feminism and feminist therapy and to discuss the ethical concerns with which each confronts the others. First, I will outline some of the difficulties which confront women in terms of their emotional and psychological development and the handicaps which have to be overcome along the road to achieving maturity. Feminists and family therapists will punctuate this description differently, but an understanding of the differential development of women and men needs to be considered as the primary background material from which decisions can reasonably be made in selecting an effective therapeutic approach and in considering its ethical imperatives.

First the mother–daughter relationship. This has been explored in detail by feminist writers, by psychoanalysts (Flax, 1978) and by family therapists (Carter and McGoldnick, 1980; Walters *et al.*, 1981). The difficulties which females experience in relation to their mothers and within their own mother–daughter relationships appear to be qualitatively different from those experienced by boys. They do not in fact seem to have a complete parallel in the difficulties which boys experience either in relation to their mothers or to their fathers. Many different reasons can be advanced in explanation: the mother still holds the main and primary caretaking role and so carries the main responsibility for giving and witholding nurturance and therefore the main responsibility when things go wrong. As Bowlby (1969) points out, mothers identify strongly with their female children. The reproduction of a being that is wholly like the self has less incongruence and strangeness about it than the reproduction of difference. But by the same token, it seems more difficult for the mother to achieve a clear sense of differentation between herself and a daughter and thus it is more difficult for her to help her baby daughter to move from what Klein (1952) describes as the early paranoid-schizoid position of complete fusion with the mother to the depressive position, when the baby begins to perceive herself as different from mother, within a world of whole, separate objects. Stemming from this early phase, the mother-daughter relationship, according to Chodorow (1978), becomes therefore one of 'prolonged symbiosis and overidentification'. Moreover in order to move to the next stage in her development, out of infancy and into childhood, the little girl has to 'give up' her close survival relationship with her primary caregiver, whose image she mirrors, and relate instead to father who is normally at this stage in the child's development a more distant figure, and is certainly someone who is 'other' and 'different' from what she is.

By contrast, the baby boy can move from being fused with mother and nurtured by her into his first experience of a sexual relationship with her. The relationship with mother cannot of course be fulfilled genitally – he has to experience the pain of losing out to father – but for the boy, this 'loss' of his first woman holds out the hope of a future restoration of maternal care, combined with full genital sexuality, in his adult relationships with women. In a very real sense he will be able 'to return to the womb' through his penis, and because of the social arrangements of the vast majority in our society, he will receive from his partner continuing nurturance and maternal care. He too can move from mother to father as a natural model.

The baby girl, on the other hand, has a more complex set of developmental tasks to perform. She must, like her brothers, separate out from mother if she is to become her own person. Yet, unlike her brothers, she cannot identify with her father as a stepping stone towards her own sense of personal autonomy. Moreover, her mother is likely to be more ambivalent about separating from her than she is from her son. Her daughter is a mirror of herself. She wants to hold on to her. She may want to do so *protectively*, keeping her away from the hostile ways in which the world can treat a female; or to do so *possessively* and jealously in case her daughter becomes her rival. The little girl must try to move away from closeness with her ambivalent mother and make a sexual claim upon her father. Like the boy, she has to be disappointed in this effort, but unlike the boy, the resolution of this disappointment, is, for her, a sideways move back to an identificatory relationship with the mother that she must ultimately leave. The sense of movement forward from one emotional step to the next, which characterises the normal developmental pattern of the little boy, is interrupted for the little girl by this uncertain 'return' to her primary caregiver. It is as though the little girl is posed with a choice between remaining close to her mother, which enables her to develop her identification with her own sex and retain that part of mother's good will which is based on her desire to prevent her daughter from separating. Or, on the other hand, she can choose to develop towards separation and autonomy (denied if she adopts the first course) and by so doing, risk forfeiting her need to build up and retain a strong identification with the parent of the same sex as well as risking incurring mother's disapproval and consequently the loss of her love.

Freud, Jung, Adler and their followers all deliberated on the problems of growing up female and, although psychoanalytic writers have received much criticism from feminist therapists, an attentive reading of what the founding fathers of psychoanalysis *actually said* reveals them to be often uncertain, sometimes quite baffled, but seldom hostile to the female psyche. It is of course true that the biological premise of Freud's own constructs tends to lead to the conclusion that 'anatomy is destiny' and that therefore it is difficult to change the inferior and powerless position that women so often find themselves to be in. But, despite his descriptions of such phenomena as the 'castration complex' and 'penis envy' (concepts largely abandoned by analysts today), Freud's writing on the subject of female sexuality is remarkably open-minded.

Notably Freud (1925) repeatedly asserts that 'the reactions of human individuals of both sexes are of course made up of masculine and feminine traits' (p. 339) and that as all human beings 'combine in themselves both masculine and feminine characteristics, ... pure masculinity and femininity remain theoretical constructions of uncertain content' (p. 342). Freud (1933), challenges a prevailing stereotype when he asserts that 'even in the sphere of human sexual life you soon see how inadequate it is to make masculine behaviour coincide with activity and feminine with passivity'. Sayers (1982) in fact suggests that although Freud's work undoubtedly holds deterministic constructs in its description of the female psyche, it does have important advantages over some of the critical writings of feminist theorists who abandon much that is helpful in the psychoanalytic scheme. Although Freud mainly neglects the systemic influences of both family and environment upon the development of personality, he does point up from within the *intra*-psychic situation (his chosen field of enquiry) the additional contradictions and obstacles that lie in the path of the development of the female psyche. These obstacles and contradictions include the sense of inferiority and low self-esteem with which many little girls are imbued; the equation of femininity with passivity and receptivity; their dependence upon men (fathers, husbands, sons) for ontological meaning to their life and the prescribed behaviours and attitudes which have come to be seen as inherently part of mothering. According to Sayers (1982), 'Freud advances and questions, rather than reproduces, received notions about our personal experience – our motherliness and femininity' (p.81).

By describing the picture from the little girl's point of view, I do not mean to imply, as feminist writers tend to do, that all is plain sailing, developmentally speaking, for the little boy. The little boy can experience his early fusion with mother and his separation from her as so traumatic that he may in adult life be overcome by fears of closeness with another woman as well as prevented from making a close relationship with one because he continues to fear the loss of his mother's love if he should 'abandon her' for another. The little boy may be held by the mother in an unresolved oedipal position, out of her own need to fill a vacuum left by an over-distant, hostile or absent husband. This again may prevent the little boy in adult life from forming mature sexual relationships with women and, if he tries, he may discover that he only knows how to relate to his partner as a little boy does to his mother. Or conversely, his separation from his mother and identification with his father may have been so complete that, in adult life, he finds he has lost touch with the feminine parts of his personality. They may have been repressed out of a need to be like a father whose feminine characteristics were themselves repressed, so that his masculinity is expressed through a caricature of macho aggressiveness. This type of adult male will obviously find relationships with women difficult in a different way. His need to dominate and control either through distancing manoeuvres or through violence will produce the conditions for women's experience of a patriarchal society at its worst. Devastating though this situation is for women, what feminist writers tend not to highlight is the extreme deprivation that is involved in this dysfunctional situation *for men too.* Cut off from his ability to be nurturant, receptive or vulnerable, the man becomes excluded from whole areas of emotional life and reduced to performing instrumental activities within and outside the family greatly to his own emotional impoverishment. The splitting, polarising and labelling of characteristics as male or female and all the sex stereotyping that then follows from this process is damaging to both men and women, although in different ways and, perhaps too, in different degrees. Moberley (1983), in her analysis of the roots of homosexuality, shows how failures in the process of identification with the same-sex parent create the continuing need in adult life to complete what has been left uncompleted by re-creating a close emotional relationship with someone of the same sex. Since there are at least the same numbers of male homosexuals as female homosexuals and maybe more, we may assume that men experience as much difficulty at this early infantile state, in developing a strong identification with the same sex.

But in contrast to the main thrust of Moberley's analysis, we must affirm the need for both women *and* men to develop and sustain close, intimate emotional relationships with members of their own sex. The fear of homosexuality with its roots in an over-strong separation from the parent of the same sex, cuts off many men and women from this continuing adult source of emotional gratification. Both sexes suffer from this deprivation, though it may indeed be the case that at least until the rise of the women's movement in the 1960s and 1970s and probably now too, *the need for* close emotional bonding between women is greater, because of their disadvantaged and stigmatised position. Likewise *the opportunity* for such close bonding is less than for men because they are often cut off from social intercourse and confined within the walls of the home. Moreover, close relationships between adult women are often fraught with difficulties because of the competition between women for men, deriving both from the early oedipal competition with mother and the social structures of society which prescribe 'finding a man' and if necessary fighting one's fellow women in the process as part of the normal feminine role. This experience of alienation from fellow women gave strong impetus in the early years of the women's movement to the development of self-help groups for women, consciousness-raising groups, story-telling groups and other peer-group experiences which serve to build solidarity between women and overcome their sense of isolation and alienation.

The foregoing discussion indicates that there is ample evidence to suggest that women are handicapped both psychologically, developmentally and environmentally in the task of becoming mature and fulfilled human beings. The developmental task for us is more complex than for men and the cultural expectations on us are full of contradictions. Feminist writers have succeeded in sharply highlighting these issues. The questions which must now be addressed are as follows. Has the field of family therapy shown any awareness of these insights? Has the feminist movement itself made good use of them in its therapeutic work? Has there been any cross-fertilisation between the fields of family and feminist therapy? What are the ethical implications for therapeutic work raised by these issues? Do either family or feminist therapists address these ethical considerations at all satisfactorily and of the two, do family or feminist therapists address them most fully?

I want first, however, to summarise some material relating to the practice of psychotherapy with women generally, and then to consider briefly the relationship between feminism and the field of psychotherapy as a whole before turning to the relationship between feminist therapy and family therapy.

Various pertinent sociological facts confront us when considering the therapeutic needs of and service delivery to women. For example, in Britain, four-fifths of the National Health Service patient population are women, of which many consult their doctors for psychogenic disorders of varying degrees of severity. Chesler (1971, 1972) has drawn attention to the fact that the majority of psychotherapy and psychiatric patients in Britain and the United States are female, whilst most therapists are male. She suggests that psychotherapy inflicts a sexist ideology on women by men, that the male therapist-female patient relationship replicates the husband-wife dominant-subordinate relationship as well as the down power position that women generally experience in society. The fact that such a grossly disproportionate percentage of the psychiatric patient population are women is related, according to Gore (1972), first to the specific sex and marital roles carried by men and women and second to the condition of learned helplessness which is more prevalent amongst women.

Feminist critics both within and outside the psychotherapy field have drawn attention to the overuse of psychotropic drugs, particularly with female patients. The main argument to be advanced here is that these drugs, by definition, and in common with all other symptom-removing interventions, dampen down the actute distress and pain which the patient is experiencing and thereby remove from her the impetus to change the situation that is causing the distress. The use of tranquillisers with women coping with impossible marriages, appalling housing conditions, loneliness or chronic physical abuse does not simply not help, but actively hinders the search for more appropriate change interventions. The fact that far more women present for help to all types of helping agencies make them easy targets for front-line, first-order change approaches and it therefore behoves the therapist to use caution in the practice of his initial approach to the person presenting the problem. Later in this chapter attention will be paid to the advantages of employing a systems approach and viewing the woman as presenting the problem *on behalf* of the others who make up her social and emotional network. Suffice it to say at this point that it is obviously quite unethical to regard one person as bearing the responsibility for a network of complex intra-familial and wider social problems and indicate this view by relating to her as the sole target of treatment interventions.

Brodsky (1980), in her review of a decade of feminist influence on psychotherapy, reports several interesting findings. For example, women report more satisfaction than men from psychotherapy (although it is not clear if this correlates with objective behavioural criteria for improvement); and the longest treatment relationships in psychotherapy occur between attractive young male therapists and attractive young female clients. Broverman *et al.* (1970) have suggested that therapeutic theories have usually supported rather than questioned sexual stereotyping or roles and maintained different standards of mental health for men and women. Brodsky (1980), however, comments on the enormous difficulties that have occurred in empirically demonstrating the evidence for sex bias and sex-role stereotyping in psychotherapy. Both are frequently reported by female patients, but it has not proved possible as yet to support these data statistically. Brodsky speculates from client self-reports that there is no sex-bias if the client is young, single and uncertain in her relationships with men, but sex bias *is* prevalent if she is older and/or married. Some writers suggest that there may be less sex bias than simple misinformation amongst male therapists in their dealings with women's problems. It is probably much harder than we often allow for men and women to experience a deep empathy and understanding for what it is like to have the body, social situation, role and role expectations carried by the other. Reports from the sex therapy literature do, however, show that there are quite clear imbalances in the way women and men are treated. During the physical examinations, for example, the female patient is routinely stimulated by both male and female therapists, whilst male patients are not (Hartman and Fithian, 1972). This could be accounted for by the fact that inorgasmia is a more common disorder amongst women, but inorgasmia is not the sole problem presented by female patients to sex therapists. Again, where surrogates are used, they are far more likely to be female surrogates than male. On the other hand the work of Masters and Johnson (1970) has been responsible for exploding a variety of burdensome myths regarding female sexuality which have hitherto served to handicap women's freedom and self-esteem in her sexual relationships.

Direct sexual abuse of the therapeutic relationship appears to be increasing at least with regard to psychiatrists and their patients (Roman *et al.*, 1978). Because most patients are women, this means that women are abused much more often than men. Although sexual contact is specifically prohibited for medically qualified psychotherapists, there is no comparable prohibition relating to non-medical psychotherapists. Although, theoretically the patient could have recourse to the law and/or to the therapist's professional association, in practice such action is very difficult to pursue to a successful outcome.

I shall now briefly review some of the underlying assumptions made by feminist therapists and some of the psychotherapeutic approaches favoured by them before turning to a discussion of the relation between feminism and family therapy.

Feminists hold two main attitudes towards psychotherapy. Some reject it completely as being a potent tool in the patriarchal system. They advocate instead peer support through the establishment of self-help groups which both provide opportunities for creating solidarity among women in general and give mutual support and help in relation to particular crises such as rape, abortion and pregnancy. The second group is made up of a range of women therapists who describe themselves as feminist and yet who continue their practice of psychotherapy. Thus, without abandoning the practice of formal psychotherapy, they have wished to examine the ways in which psychotherapy may itself be oppressive and their work is directed towards assessing traditional therapeutic models in the light of feminist concerns and developing tools for addressing the special problems presented by women, in particular the need to connect the inner and outer worlds of experience – the personal with the political.

Stock *et al.* (1982) suggest that 'feminism is not a new system of psycho-therapy, but rather a theoretical approach to any psychotherapy of women'. A feminist therapist therefore brings certain crucial underlying assumptions to her practice, whatever kind of psychotherapeutic approach she may be using. Stock *et al.* continue, 'Implicit is the idea that psychology involves biology, interpersonal relationships and the social roles and norms that have been established and maintained. Although individual women bring to therapy their own life histories and current problems they also bring internalised social stereotypes and values.' Amongst these will be the condition of learned help-lessness contingent upon the position of subordination and powerlessness experienced by most women. It is assumed by the feminist therapist that a woman coming into therapy will be caught into a series of complex binds which are preventing her from getting anywhere near realising her full potential. She will be suffering from low self-esteem and will frequently be victimised both within her family and in society by the operation of powerful sexual stereotyping which confines her to fixed and limited roles. Feminists regard traditional psychotherapy as value-laden and sexist and as being prone to reinforce the sexual stereotypes which exist in society (in the ways already discussed). Importantly it reinforces the hierarchical relationship between helper and helped, expert and neophyte, male and female. Feminist therapists therefore place great emphasis upon the development of a shared, egalitarian relationship with the client in which the therapist refuses to allow the client to invest her with the power and projections which usually follow from the hierarchical model. Invariably, the therapist is a woman, which allows for a variety of therapeutic possibilities. The client can experience the value of a close emotional relationship with another woman who is not ambivalent about her, like her mother or her daughter; or competitive with her as she may experience other women as being. The female therapist can role-model a more assertive attitude to life so that the client can learn to take hold of the power that is hers and begin to become aware of and make rational choices about her own needs and life goals which may have lain dormant until now.

Feminist therapists have given attention to symptomatic presentations that particularly occur amongst women such as over-eating, anorexia, drug abuse, sexual difficulties, phobias and depression. Because of the nature of some of these presenting symptoms, many feminist therapists have been attracted towards the use of behaviour therapy. Behaviour therapy has shown good results with patients suffering from phobias, over-eating and sexual difficulties and cognitive behaviour therapy has been successfully used with depressive conditions. Assertiveness training both in groups and with individuals has been widely used by feminist therapists (Jabubowski, 1977). Whatever the therapeutic method adopted by the feminist therapist, the crucial argument hinges on the idea that women's problems are significantly different from those of men and require therefore a significantly different approach. When asking the question – is psychotherapy with women different from any 'good' therapy? Stock *et al.* are bound to answer, 'Yes! For women many psychological problems are generated by a social definition of gender that promotes passivity and dependence on a narrow personal set of reinforcers. In addition to the customary skills, therapists who work with women need to be familiar with and responsive to the special problems that inhibit women's growth and development' (p. 154). To which I think one must offer a qualified 'yes ... but' in reply. Earlier in this paper I attempted to establish that women do indeed suffer from a variety of intra-psychic, inter-personal and environmental handicaps which do not burden men. And yet I believe we can as psychotherapists perceive these differences to be more significant than they really are. Feminist therapists have been instrumental in bringing to our attention crucial areas of difficulty which are especially experienced by women. This is highly relevant information for therapists working with women's problems. Yet the feminist therapist may need to heed the point made by Radcliffe-Richards (1980) in her searching discussion of feminism: 'having used new evidence to revise the old theories about women and to put forward theories of their own which they find more attractive, they (feminists) elevate them to too great a height and presume them true. Having done that, they use their new theories to dismiss any incoming evidence which conflicts with them' (p. 12). In the field of mental health with which we are concerned in this book, the 'old theories' about women certainly had to be discredited and must indeed be dismissed, but our task is to avoid replacing them simply with a new, inadequate mythology.

Feminists have made major inroads into the burdensome mythology, sexual stereotyping and stigmatisation by which women have been, and continue to be, so acutely handicapped. Obviously there are real differences between men and women in their anatomy, biochemistry and personality development. Most men, for example, are physically stronger than most women and this obvious fact leads to oppressions which are specifically female such as rape and battering. Physiological and anatomical differences are such that women must cope with the primary burdens of pregnancy and abortion. The social structures of society and of most social institutions are such that there remains widespread discrimination against women in all sorts of ways. All these contextual facts must be in the front of every therapist's consciousness when working with a female client. But it is also the case that both men and women equally, though differently, have to come to terms with insoluble existential problems, for example, the extraordinary fact that we all emerge out of the body of another. How do any of us, male or female *ever* get the relationship right between ourselves and that person – our mother – when the experience of the two parties is so strange and so unbalanced? Again, Mitchell (1974) draws attention to other complex major experiences which are common to both men and women, for example the extraordinary fact of sexuality itself. Both women and men 'live out in their mental life the great difficulty that there are men and women. Without distinction, both sexes are preoccupied with the great distinction: in different ways they both flee from its implications' (p. 50).

Moreover, there are many indications that men are as much burdened by sexual stereotyping as women – though fewer men may be conscious of this fact. Most men are still prevented by the social and institutional structures, and by the cultural norms of society, from caring for their children and from homemaking, as much as they are deprived by their biology of the experience of childbirth. More crucially, many men continue to be prevented by the prevailing cultural stereotypes from expressing emotions that are traditionally considered to be 'feminine': warmth, softness, dependency, vulnerability and grief expressed through tears. Moreover, many men suffer in families from the covert power wielded by women, who, in turn, are forced to take power covertly because this is all society allows to a woman. Men are also the victims of the power imbalance as well as the overt oppressors. One of the conundrums of modern family life is, as Golder (1985) points out, that 'women are simultaneously too powerful and socially degraded' (p.37). Both statuses have negative effects on both women and men. It may be that it is the lack of a systemic understanding of the relationship between roles and tasks that prevents feminists in their writings and in their therapy from acknowledging these other, complementary facts. It is to the systemic perspective, as it is exercised within family therapy, to which I now therefore turn.

Until recently, there was practically no meeting ground between feminism/feminist therapy and family therapy. Not until 1978 was the first paper on the relationship between the two published in one of the major family therapy journals (Hare-Mustin, 1978). This was followed by a discussion of the challenges and promises involved in the training of women as family therapists (Caust *et al.*, 1981); papers addressed to the relationship between feminism and family therapy (Libow *et al.*, 1982; Osborne, 1983; and Golder, 1985); and the work of the Women's Project in Family Therapy (Walters *et al.*, 1981) which examined the dilemma of women in families and the implications of these for family therapy. Golder's recent contribution has by far the hardest cutting edge and most of the following discussion will therefore be directed towards her work.

Considering that the relationship between women and men lies at the very heart of the family, it is a remarkable fact that family therapists have appeared to be so untouched by the feminist movement. Less remarkable perhaps is the avoidance by feminist therapists until recently of family therapy as a method of intervention. Feminism and feminist therapy has a more recent history than family therapy and much of its identity has been predicated, as we have noted, on the delineation of difference and imbalance between the sexes. Feminist ideology is based on the repudiation of the nuclear family, as the cradle from which springs the very root of sexual oppression. It is not surprising therefore that feminist therapists have been cautious about espousing a method of work which may strengthen and assist the functioning of the family group. But the avoidance of feminism by family therapists is more remarkable, for family therapy's most fundamental premise is based on the vital importance of *context*, so that this isolation from the influence of the feminist movement or of feminist therapists is hard to understand. Presumably it is because, as Kingston points out in chapter 9, our focus on context all too often means *family* context only and it may not therefore include the events and influences of the *social and political context*. Even so, as Golder (1985) comments 'this blind spot seems absolutely extraordinary when one considers the embattled condition of the contemporary family and the extent to which the battle lines have been drawn around conflicting ideologies about how gender relations should be structured ... Against this backdrop, an eerie calm pervades the pages of "Family Process"' (pp. 33–4). (And it might be added, all the other major family therapy journals too!).

The reason lies, I think, within the constraints of systems theory itself and the espousal of it by family therapists. The great leap forward, the discontinuous change from the past which the application of systems theory allows, is the way in which it enables behaviour to be conceptualised as an expressive act, related to all the behavioural acts of others within the individual's psycho-social system. Likewise, the roles and functions of one person are determined by and determine equally the roles and functions of every other member of the system. For the family therapist it is therefore an arbitrary matter as to who expresses the problems or pain, since these are understood to be expressions on behalf of the system as a whole. But this construct assumes that power *can* be (even if it actually is not) distributed equally between the sub-systems which themselves comprise a hierarchy within the system as a whole. 'In this regard, the feminist assertion that power in family life is socially structured by gender simply offends the systemic aesthetic' (Golder, 1985, p. 33). Here we reach the nub of the problem and the place where the ethical assumptions of feminism and family therapy are in open conflict. For the family therapist holds a moral commitment to the view that problems of family functioning are inextricably related to the functioning of the system as a whole, so that the 'blame-game' of the family, whereby *one member* is scapegoated for the difficulties experienced within *the system* as a whole is profoundly unfair as well as being untrue. The feminist, however, holds a moral commitment to the view that there is an essential imbalance in the power and position of men and women, and their relationships with each other must therefore always be affected by this fact whatever else is going on within the system in which they are embedded. To the feminist, the family therapists' concept of circular causality looks like a more sophisticated version of holding the raped or battered woman as in some sense 'responsible' for what has happened to her. The ethical stance of the feminist comes from a firm alliance made with the weaker, disadvantaged party, which is, in the feminist's view, always the woman. The ethical stance of the family therapist however, is based on the belief that there are no victims – and to argue that there are is always an oversimplification. Neither argument seems to me to be conclusive without reaching over and adopting some constructs from the other. For example, the problem with the feminist position is that it is manifestly untrue to the family therapist that the victim is always the woman. The family therapist, who is in a position to see family and marital relationships in interaction before him, naturally has the possibility of different (i.e. empirical) data to draw on. On the other hand, because most family therapists in practice, if not in theory, confine their attention to the family system and ignore the influences of the wider social and political context, they are in danger of ignoring the fact that one of the attributes of being a woman in a family is that the gender role itself carries with it an intrinsic degree of powerlessness – which may be and often is converted into covert power but which remains problematic in different ways both for men and for women. One yardstick we can use is the comparative mental health of men and women in marriage. There is, for example, ample evidence (Gore and Tudor, 1973; Bachrach,1975; Roddoff, 1975) to show that marriage produces higher levels of mental health (compared with singleness) for men but lower levels of mental health for women, but this fact is mainly ignored by the family therapist when making her assessment of an individual marriage or family situation. Whilst feminists tend to view women always and men never as the sufferers, which, from a family therapist's perspective, is highly simplistic and inaccurate, the family therapist tends to regard family members' potential for presenting problems as being broadly equal, which does not accord with the facts. And the facts, the feminist would argue, are apparent for all to see, if the family therapist would only attend to the influences within the wider system.

The family therapist's myopia does not stop short at theory. Golder points out the confused and ambiguous nature of the family therapy session itself in relation to the family therapist's attitude towards the sex roles of family members. It is usually the woman, mother, who initiates therapy. She is the member with whom the therapist must form an initial alliance in order to gain entry into the family system at all. She is the gateway to the family and very often too the gateway to communications within the family. Frequently therefore the therapist is put in a position of using mother covertly to gain entry and to help the family remain in therapy, whilst at the same time reducing her power and encouraging her to make drastic changes in the way she handles the children/relates to her husband/mother, etc., or whatever changes the specific family dynamics may require.

In other words, we utilise the very centrality we challenge, we rely on the very traits of character we critique and in essence, without realising it, we exploit women's helpless social position, all in the service of gaining therapeutic leverage. This opportunistic stance operates at many levels, but at bottom it reduces to the fact that women are typically more willing to change, so family therapists push them harder (Golder 1985, p. 41).

We might add too that women usually have far fewer choices in the matter. Because of their central position in family life and the fact that they often have no other role than those conferred by their family membership, they *need* the family to succeed more than the male members do. Men have more opportunities for escape – into their work, into places where men can go alone and women still cannot, into other relationships and, if necessary, from the family altogether. Moreover, the consequences of family and marital break-up are far more catastrophic for women than for men. The loss of social role and status, the reduction in the family's finances, the burdens of child-rearing and single parenthood are usually all experienced more severely by women than by men after the break-up of a marriage. Women therefore typically have more at stake, and will therefore risk much more, when it comes to entering therapy and embarking on the painful and risky business of trying to change family relationships.

Family therapists are as much prey to sexual stereotyping and deeply internalised prejudices as anyone else. We have all been brought up in a patriarchal society where inherited attitudes towards gender roles determine the ways in which we regard women and men. For example, I was taken aback by my own sense of surprise when I read Collier's comment in chapter 8 on his male colleague's new hair-do! In training to do family therapy, such prejudices need close attention and are given in some training programmes (Piercy *et al.*, 1983). But in strategic family therapy training programmes, where no attention is paid to the personality or personal growth of the therapist, there is no opportunity for even becoming aware of the problem. Brodsky (1980) found that many therapists working in individual psychotherapy were unwilling to admit they have any bias regarding gender issues, much less consider what to do about them. There is no reason for supposing that family therapists are any different.

The structuring of our own relationships as therapists too has impact on the family's own political organisation, a fact to which we pay far too little attention. The discussion of therapist gender in the family therapy literature has been mainly confined to the pragmatic issues of whether a male or female therapist (or a heterosexual co-therapy pair) is best suited to achieving the goals of therapy (Dowling, 1979; Sonne and Lincoln, 1965; Skynner, 1976). For example, can a female therapist identify more easily with mother and, by entering into a mothering relationship with her, supplant the negative influences of mother's real mother on the marriage? Can a male therapist role-model for a shy and dependent husband, aspects of masculinity which would enable him to take a stronger and more potent line with regard to his children, as well as providing him with more confidence in his sexual relationship with his wife? But as we review ways in which we have directed our thinking about gender role-models, it is easy to see how the wider issues of sexual politics have usually been disregarded. For example, family therapists frequently talk about the usefulness of a heterosexual co-therapy pair acting as role models in marital therapy. But how often do we reflect upon the effects of the actual structural relationship of the typical therapeutic pairing which we offer to the family – a female social worker working with a male psychiatrist? However excellent the quality of their relationship, the structurally less powerful position of the female reflects the structurally less powerful position of the wife. The female therapist may be, and often is, more competent and skilful than her male colleague, just as the wife may possess greater competence and skill both inside and outside the family group. However, when the chips are down, both the male therapist and the husband have structural advantages which derive from their position within the *supra-system of society* and yet which profoundly, even though implicitly, affect the system of *family group plus therapist team*.

The fact that family therapists have all but ignored the supra-system in respect of gender issues parallels the many other ways in which they have ignored supra-system issues, a matter discussed further by Kingston in chapter 9. The consequences for gender relationships are the same as those which relate to health and unemployment. If the family therapist ignores the structural influences that impinge on the family from its environment, he or she is left tinkering with the nuts and bolts of family relationships when the relationships between men and women in society as a whole are in severe disarray. He is left doing a patching up job, or, worse still, intervening in the wrong system.

Yet, *because* the family therapy situation almost always entails a meeting ground between men and women struggling with problems of mutual concern, we have opportunities which therapists working in other therapeutic modalities simply do not have. This is clearly illustrated by the position adopted by the feminist therapist. The ethical problems raised by the way in which the family therapist ignores sexual politics are severe, but the feminist therapist's approach runs into different ethical difficulties which, if she were to have regard to a more systemic perspective, she might avoid. The first major difficulty stems from the fundamental assumption upon which feminist therapy rests. Almost all feminists practise individual therapy, and they operate therapeutically from within a stance of strong and expressed partiality. If they hold extreme feminist views and indeed have experienced severe oppression themselves from men both inside and outside the family, the feminist therapist is likely to encourage in her client the idea (which she probably holds already) 'that maleness can be used as a criterion for badness' (Radcliffe-Richards, 1980, p. 13). It is very comfortable, but usually rather ineffective, to side wholeheartedly with one's client's prejudices, however experientially reasonable they may seem to be. Prejudice is always more murky and more complex than the labelling process allows. When we attend to the individual client's membership of her family system, the family therapist confronts the feminist on unequivocally ethical grounds. For there is strong evidence to suggest (Gurman and Kniskern, 1978) that administering continuous therapeutic inputs into one family member who is experiencing relationship difficulties, frequently serves to disrupt the relationship system in unpredictable and often destructive ways. The feminist therapist, like other individual therapists, would claim that that is not her concern. She might, because of her negative views about family and marital relationships, claim that this would be a beneficial side-effect of her therapeutic work. But it raises the question as to whether, given that it has now been well established by empirical research that relationships suffer from individual therapy, the feminist therapist has the right to her partiality or to intervene practically in such a way as to damage the interests of those who are not within her therapeutic orbit. Does she, for example, make clear to her client at the outset of therapy that, by becoming more assertive (obviously very laudible in its own right) her client's relationship with those who are living with her will be changed? Unless they are invited to become involved in the therapy, her client's gain is very likely to be loss for the other family members, instead of the *mutual* gain that it could well be.

It is the contention of this paper that more moral dilemmas are involved in the feminist therapist's position than in the family therapist's avoidance of feminist concerns. This does not mean that I think the latter unimportant; on the contrary, they are vital and the deficiencies of family therapists in this area should be addressed forthwith. Moreover, this could, I believe, be done by a relatively simple programme of re-education in the following ways. First, the family therapist in training and continually throughout practice should examine the roots of his or her own gender prejudice, becoming progressively aware of and able to alter his or her own tendencies towards sexual stereotyping. This would mean that family therapy training programmes should assume sex bias in their trainees and take active steps to eradicate it. Second, family therapists should learn more sociology. The gap between family therapy theory and the field of family studies remains wide and there is little evidence to show that family therapists pay any rigorous attention to research into the changing roles of women and men in society or to employment patterns, poverty, ethnicity or patterns of mental health and mental illness specific to the culture in which they are working. All too often, the family for the family therapist remains a closed system and this has crucial repercussions on the way in which the family therapist handles matters of eco-systemic politics within the internal political structures of the family. Third, the family therapist needs to pay more attention to the idiosyncratic features of individual family members. The fact that the family works like a special type of social system need not preclude attention to specific, non-transferable characteristics that belong to each member of that system. This would enable the family therapist to take a more realistic view of the part that gender plays in the available choices and change potential within the power structure of the family. Fourth, the family therapist should pay more attention to the feminist therapist's emphasis on a shared, egalitarian relationship with the client. This would involve developing experiential, existential and client-centred approaches to family therapy instead of the hierarchical, distancing approaches of the strategic school. Although Libow *et al.* (1982) suggest that feminist therapists should use family therapy to break out of the traditional stereotypes of the helping professions, 'the reactive and expressive aspects of the so-called feminine role', and adopt instead the directive, proactive and instrumental stance of the strategist, we may hope that the influence will act the other way round. Finally, we may hope too that family therapists will make use of the moral and ethical potential of the family therapy situation and use their unique position to influence the politics of the family in such a way that a non-sexist, egalitarian and participative culture can be established, both inside the family group and beyond.

6

'FAMILY THERAPISTS ARE POTENTIALLY DAMAGING TO FAMILIES AND THEIR WIDER NETWORKS.' DISCUSS

Andy Treacher

At the time I first began to collect my ideas together to write this chapter I was also marking the scripts of third-year psychology students sitting an exam in clinical psychology that I had set them. The hypothetical question (that gives this chapter its title) popped into my brain at that time. But sadly it is unlikely that this type of question will be set either now or in the future. Such a woolly question as this would be frowned upon by the average examination board, but I think it *is* time that family therapists set themselves the task of examining their ethical and political stances more openly and more directly and begin to ask themselves this type of question.

Such self-examination is becoming all the more urgent because family therapy runs the risk of becoming both fashionable and successful. The publication of their very successful book, *Families and How to Survive Them* by Robin Skynner and his superstar ex-client John Cleese (1983), perhaps marks a new stage in the process of establishing family therapy. The process of professionalisation is far advanced in America where family therapy is now big business, and leading family therapists can demand enormous fees for their services. Britain lags behind, but all the signs indicate that a new profession will begin to emerge in the near future.

As Pilalis has pointed out in a recent paper (1984) the process of professionalisation raises important issues about who 'owns' specialised knowledge. Organisations (such as the Association for Family Therapy) which are initially formed to promote the development and communication of knowledge can become barriers to its wide dissemination. This process would be extremely ironic as far as family therapy is concerned since it is a body of knowledge that has borrowed from a wide range of other bodies of knowledge. The impetus to 'professionalise' is understandable in terms of the desire of practitioners to gain higher status for family therapy knowledge, but if professionalisation does occur then an elite group of highly trained family therapists may well emerge – they may then seek to claim that they (and only they) are to use the term 'family therapist' since they alone are sufficiently well qualified to undertake family therapy.

The implications of such a development is wide ranging but it is inevitable that potential clients would suffer. Illich's challenging work on the disabling effects of professions (Illich and McKnight, 1977) would come home to roost with a vengeance and family therapy would be seen as yet another disabling profession. Eventually the 'Association for Family Therapy' would actually become a misnomer – the true title would have to be the 'Association for Family *Therapists*'. The prime goal of the Association would then hinge around protecting the professional needs of family therapists rather than meeting the needs of their clients. Family therapy would become an increasingly esoteric body of knowledge suitably dressed up in the most scientistic language possible in order to prevent non-specialists from being able to approach the subject with any feelings of competence.

Pilalis's work is a timely warning that unless family therapists put their house in order then these destructive processes will inevitably destroy family therapy as a potentially radicalising influence within the caring professions. At present the training of family therapists in this country is a chaotic mess, but the introduction of formal training programmes will not necessarily solve the problem. Formal training programmes tend to produce practitioners who jealously guard their knowledge and seek to maximise separateness from practitioners in similar professions. Formal training is normally justified by professionals because it is supposed to create professionals who internalise high standards of conduct – through a process of self-monitoring they are meant to control their own behaviour so that they always act in the best interests of their clients. Ironically research by, for example Bucher and Stelling (1977), has demonstrated that formal education programmes tend to create barriers to control by colleagues.

At first sight it may well seem that family therapy is immune to many of these effects. The increasingly widespread use of one-way screens and videotape in both training and everyday practice means that family therapists' work has a remarkably high degree of visibility when compared, for instance, with many traditional ways of undertaking therapy. But this high degree of visibility does not necessarily mean that the interests of clients are safeguarded. Because of the vagaries of current training methods in this country family therapists tend to be trained in markedly different ways – the content of a given training course is usually totally dependent on the particular 'school' to which the training staff belong. So there is little chance that a trainee will actually be exposed to a full range of family therapy techniques. This means, in fact, that there is a great deal of 'in-breeding' – trainees emerge from course and training experience with valuable skills but their knowledge of family therapy is objectively very limited. They tend to adhere to the 'school' of therapy in which they have been trained, and tend not to be sympathetic to alternative ways of work. This process is not helped by the fact that the various 'gurus' of family therapy who jet into Britain in order to hold their often dazzling and stimulating one-off workshops are not at all interested in helping to develop an integrated method that draws on the strengths of the different schools of family therapy.

If we are to take Pilalis's work seriously then family therapy as a movement is entering a potentially dangerous stage. As this new profession crystallizes, it is particularly important to worry about the impact that this process of professionalisation will have on the families that are going to be treated by future family therapists. Pilalis has quite correctly raised a number of important issues about the way that family therapy knowledge may become privatised and will not permeate the caring profession as it has in the past. I am especially worried about the possible dangers of a knowledge gap developing between family therapists and the families with which they work.

In my plenary address to the AFT conference at York in September, 1984 (Treacher, 1986), I argued that there seems to be a general rule that as caring professions emerge and begin to establish themselves as separate entities, they tend to distance themselves from the very people they are meant to be helping. I think that this is particularly true of medicine and I have attempted to utilise some of David Armstrong's work on the doctor/patient relationship (Armstrong, 1982) in order to establish this point. As medicine became 'scientific', and its monopoly over medical knowledge and medical practice became more established in the period following the Medical Registration Act of 1858, patients became increasingly invisible as people with lives and problems that were contingent on the social context in which they lived. Doctors became interested in the patients as symptom bearers and it was symptoms that became the object of the doctor's gaze.

In family therapy I think we are beginning to see the emergence of a similar trend which above all else stresses the technicality of the task the family therapist has to carry out. In my opinion it is the strategic schools of family therapy that are particularly prone to make this type of error since they adopt a highly pragmatic approach to achieving change. Strategic therapists have undoubtedly made important contributions to the development of family therapy, and I would not want to argue otherwise, but it is nevertheless important that we examine the ethical and political stances adopted by them.

Pilalis is particularly concerned with one aspect of this general issue – the importance of accountability – but her concept tends to stress the issue of peer-group accountability, while I am equally concerned with exploring the issue of the family therapist's accountability to the families that he or she has in therapy. In this brief chapter it would be impossible for me to examine the work of all the schools of strategic family therapy, but in this country strategic therapy is best known through the highly creative work of Brian Cade at the Family Institute, Cardiff. Cade acknowledges that his therapeutic style has been profoundly influenced by strategic therapists such as Haley (and hence Milton Erickson), Watzlawick, and his colleagues at the Brief Therapy Centre of the Mental Research Institute, Palo Alto, and Selvini Palazzoli and her colleagues from Milan.

The essence of Cade's approach to therapy can be most easily communicated by considering the following paragraph from a recent paper (Cade, 1984, p. 4)

> My early interpretations of Haley's work led me into construing therapy as a kind of contest in which paradoxical techniques were power tactics that could be used to prevent a client or family using symptomatic behaviour to control and define their relationship with me. Later, paradoxical work became more of an intellectual exercise, a kind of chess game. Attempts would be made meticulously to construct interventions with all potential 'loopholes' blocked, thus forcing the client or family to move outside of the rule governed symptomatic game without end, which up to that moment had no meta rules for the change of its own rule (see Watzlawick *et al.*, 1967, p. 237).

More recently Cade's work has shifted its emphasis away from using paradoxical techniques because he and his team of co-workers came to believe that it was the therapist's ability to create the unexpected in therapy that was decisive in producing change ...

> More time was spent attempting to ascertain how the client or family were expecting or apparently wanting us to be, and then taking a position or making a response ... that was isomorphic enough to connect ... yet with sufficient unexpected, sometimes absurd, even shocking elements to introduce difference (Cade, 1984, p. 2).

But Cade's position can be summarised even more succinctly than this – he quotes an aphorism of Palazzoli's which puts the whole approach in a nutshell.

> People are most influenced when they expect a certain message and receive instead a message at a totally different level ... anything predictable is therapeutically inefficient (Palazzoli, 1981, p. 45).

Palazzoli's position is particularly fascinating since it helps us understand why strategic therapists are especially gratified when their clients change behaviour during the course of therapy, and yet do not attribute their changed behaviour to any of the interventions that the therapist has made (Cade, 1984, p. 23). If therapy is a power struggle between the family and the therapist then the ideal form of therapy is one that takes place both outside of family members' consciousness and under the therapist's control. If the family knew what was happening to it then they would be able to anticipate what the next step would be and hence continue to sabotage it.

There was a time, particularly during my period of training with Brian Cade at the Family Institute, when I was happy to adopt a similar ethical stance to the one adopted by strategic therapists. Families in distress who come into therapy are in some sense customers for change – surely there is nothing wrong, therefore, in achieving change by means which are not necessarily known to the families concerned. But I have always objected to the use of psychotropic drugs in 'curing' so-called psychiatric illnesses because the 'solution' involved is opportunist and does not allow the clients involved to gain genuine control over the processes that caused the problems in the first place. How then could I at the same time support a form of therapy which was essentially similar to a particular potent form of medical treatment which effectively depoliticises any of the human issues involved?

Fortunately I am not alone in having second thoughts about strategic work. Recently, David Calof published a very thought-provoking case study in *Family Therapy Networker* (a house journal of American family therapists which often raises crucial political and ethical issues relevant to family therapy). The case history Calof presents was first written in 1977 but was not published at that time. The report describes an extremely successful piece of Ericksonian hypnotherapy undertaken with a husband and wife whose marriage was at the point of breakdown. On his own admission, Calof insists that the therapy was an extended ego trip.

> At the time I saw this couple I was a young, lay-hypnotherapist swept away with the idea of hypnosis as the great panacea. I placed great emphasis on disguised, tricky varieties of techniques while hoping never to be caught by my clients in the act of attempting to change them. I sometimes saw clients as consciously stupid and not to be trusted except unconsciously. Consequently in the case report . . . I was primarily interested in portraying my rather flamboyant, grandiose, and manipulative technique, *while the client's behaviour and resources remain as background* (Calof, 1984, p.p. 52–53 – emphasis added).

It is extremely rare for therapists to write so frankly about their work so we must be grateful to Calof for his bravery in breaking the usually accepted professional norm that is involved when therapists write up their case studies.

But Calof is by no means involved in a piece of public breast beating. His purpose is far more serious than that, since he seeks to link his change in therapeutic style to changes in his own life, as the following further quotation reveals.

> Milton Erickson was unquestionably the model for the kind of therapist I wanted to be. I was attempting to imitate and emulate Erickson ... trying to disregard myself in favour of a persona of seeming invincibility and invulnerability. At various times Dr Erickson had, like my father, terrified, confused, frustrated and nourished me. He had powerfully elicited my love, envy and respect. Certainly it is no coincidence that following Dr Erickson's death, I began taking steps to rejoin my family and to end a decade-long, chilly stand-off with my father (Calof, 1984, p. 53).

Calof's presentation reads almost like one of the fables so beloved of his mentor Erickson. 'Once upon a time there was a young man who wished to apprentice himself to a magician, but being an apprentice magician had its pitfalls ...' I should hasten to add, however, that my purpose is not to demean Calof in any way. Indeed my intention is the reverse of this. He raises many crucial issues here – one that always fascinated me concerns the reason why some therapists are almost instinctively drawn to adopting paradoxical or defiance-based interventions, while other therapists are drawn towards using more direct methods. Calof gives us a clue to possible answers in the next two paragraphs of his article in which he points out which crucial aspects of the case he actually neglected in favour of his passion for technique.

> It is clear to me now that (back in 1977) ... I regarded the couple's relations with their families of origin and parenting issues as largely irrelevant. Transgenerational and systems issues, patterns and themes were reduced in the report to mere problems with in-laws, mere differences in parenting styles, communication gaps and the like. The main focus was on the therapist's technique.
>
> I am less interested in technique today. In fact I now view any need I may have to perform or use tricky technique as more my own need than something required by the clinical situation. While I am proud of this case as an early example of my work, I wouldn't be satisfied with it today because of the authoritarian, therapist centred, manipulative style (Calof, 1984, p. 53).

I find Calof's explanation of his changed position both fascinating and tantalising because it opens up a whole new series of intriguing questions. For instance, is there a possible link between the style of therapy adopted by a therapist and the therapist's personal history? Would it be possible to explain therapists' attraction to strategic ways of working (which place a premium on distancing therapists from their clients) in terms of their formative experiences in their families of origin?

Unfortunately these questions detract from an examination of the ethical issues that are central to my concern – a major empirical study needs to be undertaken in order to establish whether there is indeed a link between therapists' personal histories and the style of therapy that they adopt. But if we pursue the ethical issues directly, then we can, I think, glean the following major insight from Calof. It seems that his shift in attitude, which led him to shun technique in favour of tackling more existential issues in therapy, was associated with important changes in his personal life. One striking feature of many strategic therapists is their studied disinterest in the personal histories of therapists, and their own in particular. Haley himself is notorious for his vigorous dismissal of personal work by therapists as being totally unnecessary for their development as therapists. I suspect that the position of the Brief Therapy Centre group at the Mental Research Institute, Palo Alto, is very similar – indeed it is significant that one member of the group, Richard Fisch (who was commissioned by the editor of the *Networker* to comment on Calof's paper), totally ignores the main thrust of Calof's paper. Fisch concentrates his attention on reviewing the pros and cons of Calof's hypnotherapy technique and advising on how he can write up a case history in greater detail so that other therapists can benefit from his approach (Fisch, 1984).

At first sight Fisch's myopia is a little bewildering, since the Brief Therapy Centre's work has contributed so much to the issue of clarifying and enhancing the 'customerhood' of clients, but I think this fact is best understood as a surface phenomenon – the essential thrust of the approach is to concentrate on the *therapist's* contribution to the equation that constitutes therapy. I am not clear where the Milan group stand in relation to personal work, but it is clear from what they have so far published that they pay very little attention to issues that concern the nature of the therapist's personal history.

To return to the main issue in relation to strategic forms of therapy. If change can only be produced by interventions that require the client either to defy the intervention that is being made or to respond to the intervention at an unconscious level, then there are very real dangers that the approach becomes totally manipulative. The ethical justification for such interventions hinges around the assumption that families can *only* change if such techniques are used. Now there is, of course, an empirical objection to this position. How does a dyed-in-the-wool strategic worker who consistently (and inflexibly) uses the type of techniques outlined above know whether or not a family that he has in therapy is capable of changing in response to direct, openly negotiated interventions? If the therapist's tactics always rely on avoiding the obvious, then the family is never given a chance to demonstrate its flexibility.

An illustration from my own case load will, I hope, serve to demonstrate how ludicrous it can be to pursue the complicated when the simple will do. A 3½-year-old girl was referred to me because of persistent soiling. A previous therapist had failed to produce any change using straightforward behavioural methods so the parents were in some despair by the time I met with them. To cut a long story short, the crucial 'intervention' which seemed to produce a breakthrough in the case was my suggestion that the parents should build a step so that their child could actually use an adult toilet without their being involved. (The child was quite small and could not sit herself on a full-sized toilet without their help.) Their anxiety about their child not defecating had resulted in them being over-involved – their anxiety made the child anxious – and so on. So in the end the 'solution' was an up-turned washing up bowl which the child used as a step which gave her enough height to be able to sit on the toilet by herself. I have deliberately used this example because it is currently fashionable for family therapists to write up cases in the family therapy journals which involve consummately skilful interventions. My case illustrates the reverse – I needed three sessions of detailed work with the parents (and their co-operation in undertaking several detailed monitoring tasks between sessions) before the solution emerged. It was as much *their* solution as it was mine, so I felt that all the work that I had undertaken with this family had been contractually established and that therapy ended with feelings of mutual respect.

It is difficult to see how strategic family therapy can be considered contractual in the same sense. I suppose it is possible to attempt to recover the situation by saying that there's an *implicit* contract involved in this type of work. The fact that the family arrives at therapy sessions at all implies that they do indeed want to change – we are therefore given carte blanche as to the means we are going to use to help them change in the direction they indicate. This type of argument is customarily used in medical situations – the doctor knows best but even here there is an assumption that the doctor should be able to explain what he is going to do if the patient has the temerity to ask. The strategic therapist would undoubtedly be in a difficult position if his clients began to question him in the same way. A counter tactic would have to be devised by the therapist and his back-up team in order to ensure that the request did not sabotage the therapy.

It is this crucial necessity for the therapist to remain phoney that is so worrying – do the family and the therapist ever relate to each other in open and frank ways, as fellow human beings? Obviously not – if therapy is a power struggle that the therapist must win for change to occur then there is no room for sentimentality or for retaining the normal type of respect that a therapist has for his or her clients. But if this traditional form of respect for clients is abandoned, what is left to guide the strategic therapist? Many theorists, I think, would agree that a family in therapy operates in the way it does because it is stuck and fearful of change (Feldman and Pinsof, 1982) – the family is typically at a point of transition in its life cycle so the future is unclear and threatening. Family members genuinely seek solutions to their problems but their repertoire of potential behaviours is limited by the constraints that have built up as a family life has come to centre around problem behaviours. The family's apparent controlled and controlling (often highly patterned) behaviour reflects its 'unfreedom' to change and develop.

Strategic therapists, in order ethically to justify their therapeutic stance, must insist that since it is unconscious processes that bind the family members together, preventing them from growth and development, interventions must be made in such a way that the family is unable to respond to the interventions except in the direction dictated by the therapist. Another British strategic therapist, Sebastian Kraemer, has recently put the strategic therapist's view most succinctly and most bluntly.

> The relatively primitive processes of human groups ... have the same inevitability as physiological and evolutionary events; they just happen. Sometimes it is useful to think of a family group as if it were an animal, just carrying on the way animals do. When, for whatever reason, it cannot carry on in the ordinary way, help is required to move the block. Just as an untamed animal is not grateful or co-operative when a human tries to rescue it from a trap, or take a thorn from its paw, so the family is not organised to 'receive' therapy which is obviously so artificial and embarrassing compared to the regular gatherings of social life. The sooner these meetings are over, and the sooner forgotten, the better (Kraemer, 1983, p. 10).

Kraemer's use of metaphor is very intriguing. I do not think it is an accident that he selects the 'family as an animal' analogy from a wide range of possible alternatives. If the family is a dangerous animal then the therapist, of course, needs to be all-powerful and to treat the family as a dangerous adversary. Such an argument therefore creates an implicit ethical justification for the therapist being extremely powerful and calculating in his approach to therapy.

Cade has offered a different reason for adopting a strategic approach.

> As with most major British cities, Cardiff is fairly cosmopolitan, and referrals to the Institute come from all social classes and reflect a wide range of cultural standards. Breunlin, Cornwell and Cade (1983) have examined some of those facets of British culture that have influenced our tendency towards the more indirect approaches to therapy. The British tend to be much more cautious about change, suspicious about 'technical' solutions to

family and other social problems, and more pessimistic about the potential outcome of 'talking' as a way of approaching problems. As Breunlin, *et al.* (1983) have observed: ... the American tendency to 'let it all hang out' and to form personal relationships quickly is regarded by the British as a sign of superficiality, transience, and egotism, and even as a breach of etiquette. The British value 'keeping oneself to oneself'. When a problem exists, it should be handled within the family, as it is important 'not to wash one's dirty laundry in public'. The British are far less direct about their inter-personal relationships, seldom making direct statements about how they function or how they wish them to be different. They maintain a 'proper' distance when relating, and avoid strong display of affect (Cade, 1984, p. 99).

Cade is half-aware that his position is very shaky, since his very next sentence comments on the fact that what he has said 'represents a rather drastic over-simplicification of British society and values'! But this comment does not stop him from producing the prize *non sequitur* that '(my discussion) can offer a useful backdrop (sic) against which to view the attitudes of the average British family towards the idea of psychotherapy'.

Of source the notion of an 'average' British family is a nonsensical sociological abstraction and I think Cade is aware of this difficulty because he hastily covers his tracks by adding 'there will, of course, be differences between various sub-cultures yet it can generally be expected that most families will demonstrate this backdrop of cultural injunctions against the openness etc. required in the process of psychotherapy'.

Interestingly, Minuchin and Fishman, who are advocates of a much more direct and manifestly overt form of family therapy (structural family therapy) have explored very similar ground to Cade. But they do so in order to explain how their form of therapy can be custom-built to suit a wide range of different types of family who can be expected to enter therapy. Minuchin and Fishman (1981, pp. 28–49) are markedly more dialectical in their discussion than Cade, who never really examines the interactive nature of the relationship between the family and the therapist. For Cade there is a simple equation that can be put as crudely as 'American culture generates "openness" therefore more open methods of family therapy can be used. British culture generates "closedness" therefore strategic methods have to be used.'

Of course it is a moot question how the Italian School of Palazzoli is to be fitted into this equation. Italian families conform to a cultural stereotype of passionate expression of emotion and yet the Milan method is one of the 'coolest' and most distancing methods of undertaking therapy – the therapist spends virtually all her time questioning the family in a rigorous and methodical way, with the therapist's back-up team being responsible for making interventions which are often designed to prevent the family from inducting the therapist into their way of responding and viewing the world.

One final point needs to be made before leaving this topic. In his presentation Cade fails to discuss the issue of *Welsh* families. Cardiff is dubbed a cosmopolitan city (which it is) but it is singularly absent-minded of Cade not to explore whether Welsh families are in any way different from English families. Breunlin, an American, is equally at fault in not drawing attention to the fact that there really is no such thing as an 'American' family. McGoldrick's recent book *Ethnicity and Family Therapy* (McGoldrick, Pearce and Giordano, 1982) has made a valuable contribution to correcting the stereotype of the 'American' family, but I do not think it is an accident that we find strategic family therapists making this type of error. Their tendency to concentrate so heavily on the therapists's contribution to the process of therapy can be expected to make them insensitive to salient differences in the families they treat.

Interestingly Peter Hudson (a one-time colleague of Brian Cade's at the Family Institute) is one of the few British family therapists to explore the necessity for modifying therapy to suit the 'style' of the family in therapy. In his article called 'Different strokes for different folks: a comparative examination of behavioural, structural and paradoxical methods in family therapy' (Hudson, 1980), he compares three major methods of family therapy and establishes that all three have a contribution to make. Other therapists, such as Stanton (1980) have argued that structural and strategic approaches can be combined in treating the same family but it is important to stress that at least one model (the McMaster model) has been explicitly developed to combine the strengths of several different models. The approach places great emphasis on skilled assessment of the family prior to making an effort to produce change – it therefore contains a very strong 'custom building' element which helps to avoid the family and the therapist getting stuck on agendas which have not been mutually negotiated.

Cade's assertion that all families are alike and all cases should be treated using strategic family therapy appears increasingly dogmatic and indefensible if it is compared with these approaches. But Cade himself can help us to understand just how such a strange situation can arise. In his recent paper (Cade, 1984) he provides us with an explanation of how individuals and families are caught up in self-fulfilling circularities. He succinctly summarises his argument by means of the diagram on page 98.

The beauty of this diagram is that it can legitimately be applied to any relatively 'closed' group, so we could, in fact, apply it to the workings of a family therapy team or institution including Cade's own situation within the Family Institute. All professional workers tend to be caught up in these types of circularities, but I think it is true to say that some professional settings are more open than others to different types of input and the close-knit structure of many strategically oriented family therapy teams seems to militate against openness to ideas emanating from other schools of therapy.

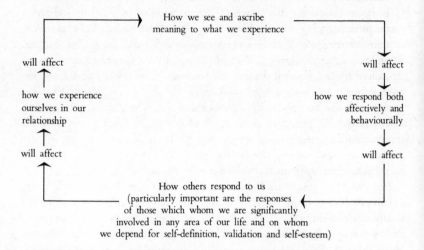

How we see and ascribe
meaning to what we experience

will affect

will affect

how we experience
ourselves in our
relationship

how we respond both
affectively and
behaviourally

will affect

will affect

How others respond to us
(particularly important are the responses
of those which whom we are significantly
involved in any area of our life and on whom
we depend for self-definition, validation and self-esteem)

I think the crucial error that Cade makes is derived from a one-sided interpretation of family characteristics. There is clearly some truth in the idea that families in Britain are reticent about sharing their problems at the initial point of contact with the therapist, but this fact need not be decisive in determining what sort of therapy should be utilised to help them. Cade's work, like that of so many strategic therapists, is always presented in a scientistic, ex-cathedra, style which precludes any discussion of the living relationship between the therapist and the families he has in treatment. Cade tells us that British families are reluctant to deal directly with personal matters, but he never tells us about himself and how he deals with his own problems. This, in turn, leads me to wonder about strategic therapists in general. Is it simply the case that they share a personal preference for dealing with personal problems indirectly and that they transfer their preference from this personal to their professional lives? Perhaps this is too crude an idea, but I do think it is time that strategic family therapists stopped using scientistic clap trap to conceal the moral and political values that permeate their therapy. I am attracted to structural family therapy precisely because it is an intense and direct way of dealing with family problems. It appeals to me because that's the way I attempt to deal with problems in my own family and in my own life.

It is therefore no accident that I instinctively turn to Minuchin's work in order to try and gain some clarity about the issues that Cade's work raises. Recently Minuchin and Fishman have explored a crucial issue which really lies at the root of my disagreement with Cade.

There is a disagreement within the field of family therapy on precisely how a therapist uses himself to achieve the leadership of the therapeutic system. Early theories of therapy portrayed the therapist as an objective data gatherer, but this myth has largely been discredited. Even in psychoanalysis, the understanding of the analyst's use of self in the process of counter-transference has sparked great changes in psychoanalytic theory and practice. It is probably true, Donald Meltzer writes, that any analysis which really taps the passions of the patient does the same for the analyst and promotes a development which can further his own self analysis. The necessary state for inspired interpretation is that type of internal companionship which promulgates an atmosphere of adventure in which comradeship develops between the adult part of the patient's personality and the analyst as creative scientist ... implying therapeutic possibilities for both parties to the adventure (Minuchin and Fishman, 1981, p. 30).

I suspect that most strategic therapists reading such a quote would find it totally unappealing. The sense of adventure that strategic therapists gain from their work is, I think, derived from a different source. Minuchin and Fishman argue that (at least as far as the Milan school is concerned) the relationship between the therapist and the family while appearing overtly friendly is in fact, covertly, an adversarial relationship. The creative and adventurous part of strategic work takes place in the back-up room where the therapist and the team brainstorm interventions which can then be delivered to the family who waits passively and uninvolved in the therapy room.

The whole structure of the therapy is, in fact, carefully designed so that the family can have as little control over the proceedings as possible. The therapist remains the distant 'expert' throughout the proceedings and his success is seen to be partially dependent on his ability to stay aloof from the family. The family is not encouraged in any way to have an understanding of the process that they are involved in since such knowledge would be dangerous and would prevent intervention from working.

So strategic family therapy is the most alienated form of therapy imaginable. At present there is virtually no research which enables us to understand what the felt experience of families undergoing strategic therapy must be. As yet the Milan group have not published any objective follow-up studies. Cade does cite evidence from individual case studies, but the follow-up interviewing that has taken place has been very superficial. The generally reported finding is that the family found the therapy unhelpful, although they often report significant changes in the family's behaviour.

So 'pure' strategic family therapy is a very maverick form of treatment indeed, but are the civil rights of families being abused by this approach? For instance, does a family ever give its informed consent to be treated in this type

of way? Does the family ever have a chance to say a genuine 'no' to any aspect
of the therapy? The 1981 revision of the Mental Health Act has recently raised
many similar issues in relation to the compulsory treatment of individuals
suffering from mental disorders. It is clear that the revision of the Act has
established new safeguards that curb the power of the medical profession to
take unilateral decisions about treatment. I think that it is time that family
therapists took these lessons seriously and voluntarily invited greater criticism
and examination of their work. Because of its theoretical stance, strategic
family therapy seeks to enhance the power of the therapist and therefore to
render the family compliant to interventions designed by the therapist and his
team. The model in its present form avoids establishing explicit contracts with
families, and indeed the model itself would provide an explanation of why and
how contractual work could be seen as damaging as far as inducing therapeutic
change was concerned.

Illich has used the term 'medical nemesis' to describe what he sees as a
growing tendency within contemporary medicine for doctors to behave in
superhuman ways controlling the life and death of their patients. His use of the
term is best explained by citing the following quotation:

> The Greeks saw gods in the forms of nature. For them nemesis represented
> divine vengeance visited upon mortals who impinge on those prerogatives
> the gods enviously guard for themselves. Nemesis is the inevitable
> punishment for inhuman attempts to be a hero rather than a human being.
> Like most abstract Greek nouns nemesis took the shape of a divinity. She
> represents nature's response to hubris, to the individual's presumption in
> seeking to acquire the attributes of a god. Our contemporary hygienic
> hubris has led to the new syndrome of medical nemesis ... Medical nemesis
> is resistant to medical care. It can be reversed only through a recovery of
> mutual self-care by the laity and the legal, political and institutional
> recognition of this right to care (Illich, 1975, p. 28).

It is a little ironic that Illich's quotation contains a reference to hubris since
the term is widely used by Palazzoli and her colleagues in their well-known
book which explores the nature of the 'schizophrenic transaction' which
permeates the behaviour of families with schizophrenic members.

> Our experience has led us to consider the state of discomfort ... (which can
> be described) ... as the consequence of a person's finding himself 'down'
> when he has tried to be up in the effort to define the relationship ... Man is
> a being who will not easily accept this kind of defeat; he will return
> compulsively to the battlefield to try again and again. He even carries on the
> same battle with God, as we are taught in the first book of Genesis, when

Adam and Eve ask why they should not eat the fruits of the tree. It is man's hubris which led to the banishment from the paradise of complementarity with his creator, which he had initially recognised and gladly accepted (Palazzoli, Boscolo, Prata and Cecchin, 1978, p. 24).

But this self-same hubris is what Palazzoli and her colleagues use to explain the pattern of never-ending conflict which characterises the behaviour of a couple who are caught up in a schizophrenic transaction.

It is by following this line of hubris, already exaggerated by their respective original learning systems, that each member of our couple chooses a 'difficult' partner. And it is exactly because of this hubris that each wants to repeat the challenge; that each presumes to succeed.

We can observe that the positions of the two in the relationship are identical and symmetrical. Each yearns desperately to gain control of the definition of the relationship and repeatedly and compulsively tests his (sic) position, thus constantly running the risk of defeat. However, hubris, that exasperated pride, has taken up its abode in each member of the couple, and can admit no defeat (1978, p. 24).

Palazzoli's brilliant and often poetic exploration of schizophrenic families is striking and her book is probably one of the most cited in the literature of family therapy, but there is no discussion of the form of hubris that therapists could be expected to suffer from. The implicit justification for Palazzoli's approach flows from the assumption that schizophrenic families are caught up in a never-ending destructive transaction from which they cannot escape. But, as we have already noted in reviewing Cade's work, this limited justification for adopting a strategic approach has not deterred other workers from adopting strategic approaches with a wide spectrum of families. It should also be noted that the Milan group have tended to use their paradoxical approach with all the families that were referred to them. (At a recent conference in the Everyman Theatre, Cardiff in 1982, Palazzoli reported that she had modified her approach since working in a state-run clinic outside Milan, but this change in approach does not seem to have registered with many of Palazzoli's disciples in Britain.)

It seems to me that if strategic workers are prepared to make a specific argument for adopting their approach in relation to families that are highly self-destructive and hence can be seen to be their own worst enemies, then there are possibilities for justifying their approach on ethical grounds. However it still seems indefensible, that a family should be involved in therapy in such an alienated and mystifying way. Perhaps a crude analogy will help to make my point. *Candid Camera* and *This is your Life* are popular television programmes which set out to manipulate unsuspecting individuals in various ways in order to create entertainment for mass audiences. Whether they are ethically justifiable is a very moot point, but obviously the programme's dénouements (to which the unsuspecting individuals are exposed) are often extremely benign and mostly personally and financially rewarding. The television programme producers obviously 'come clean' about what they have done and the fraught relationship between the programme makers and the 'victims' is resolved as amicably as possible.

I wonder if strategic therapists would ever contemplate using a similar approach? Lorion (1978) has written interestingly about the ways in which clients' fears and anxieties about therapy can be constructively dealt with by careful 'pre-therapy' orientation sessions. I wonder what price strategic therapists would pay if they modified their approach so that they held post-therapy debriefing sessions (perhaps six months or a year after treatment has been completed?) so that they could also 'come clean' about the tactics they used and why they used them. Obviously such sessions would be very fascinating both from a theoretical and an empirical point of view because it would be possible, for example, to discover more about the felt experience of families undergoing such a maverick form of treatment. But such sessions would also provide strategic therapists with a chance to escape from the potentially damaging ethical situation in which they are caught up. But the argument does not stop there. Dr Melitta Schmideberg has commented very wryly on the effects that psychoanalysis has on analysts. In an interview published in 1978 she answered the question 'what do you think happens to the analyst over a long period of undertaking therapy with clients?' by saying 'somebody compared it to a lobotomy. They get flatter and flatter. Psychoanalysis is like sensory deprivation from the analyst's point of view' (Schmideberg, 1978, p. 30).

It would, of course, be ridiculous to propose that a similar process occurs to strategic family therapists, but nevertheless it is worth worrying about the long-term effects of being a strategic family therapist. As a structural family therapist I often have a very close relationship with the families I work with. My experience of life has been vastly enriched by this closeness and I value the two-way process of learning in which I am involved. It is difficult to see how strategic family therapists can be involved in a comparable process as the essential feedback loops which connect and reconnect the family and the therapist during the course of the therapy are missing. This point leads me to have the temerity to suggest that one of the dangerous occupational hazards of a form of therapy which is so bound up with the exploiting of the possibilities of the one-way mirror, is, ironically, narcissism.

It would only be fair to conclude this chapter by making one final point – I have attacked strategic family therapy on ethical grounds throughout this chapter, but it would be sheer hypocrisy to imply that other forms of family therapy escape criticism. Strategic family therapy poses some of the sharpest ethical dilemmas that confront family therapists but this does not mean that other schools of therapy can rest easily on their laurels. As a result of writing this chapter, and being involved in the discussions that prompted it, I am more aware of the ethical difficulties posed by my own style of working – it just happens to be easier to see the beam in one's neighbour's eye before casting the mote out of one's own (or is it vice versa?)

7

FAMILY THERAPY AND RESPECT FOR PEOPLE

Richard Lindley

... the purpose of playing, whose end, both at the first and now, was and is to hold, as 'twere, the mirror up to nature; to show virtue her own feature, scorn her own image, and the very age and body of the time his form and pressure (*Hamlet*, Act 3, scene 2).

My aim in this paper is to investigate the charge that family therapy is unethical because it violates a fundamental principle of respect for people. I wish to construe 'family therapy' in a broad sense to include not just therapy which concentrates on the system of the nuclear family and its attendant sub-systems, but the 'systems approach' in general. The approach has been well described by several British family therapists (Skynner, 1976; Walrond-Skinner, 1976; Treacher and Carpenter, 1984; and Gorell-Barnes, 1984). I here follow John Carpenter (1984). Characterising a 'systems model' in regard to understanding and treating children's problems, he writes:

> A systems model always considers the child as a member of a social group, usually, but not necessarily, the family. The family, in turn, is considered as a system in interaction with other systems, such as the neighbourhood, schools, work and social agencies. It follows that there are many possible 'target' systems for the worker's intervention: the individual child; his parents; the family group; the neighbourhood. She can also intervene at the 'interface' between two systems, for example the family and the school (Carpenter, 1984, pp. 13–14).

Although there may be some who believe that the system of the nuclear family offers a key to the solution of all psychological problems, the fact that individuals are parts of many significant systems other than the family makes it implausible to claim that the family system should be the sole focus of all therapeutic concern. However, problems arising from those who make a fetish of the nuclear family are discussed by Kingston in chapter 9.

Perhaps the most controversial practice of family therapists, from a moral point of view, and the one on which I wish to focus in this paper, is the use of therapeutic strategies which require those in therapy to remain ignorant of what is really happening. A crucial feature of such strategic therapy is that the therapist deliberately induces beliefs in the person with whom she or he is communicating, in the absence of a truth-centred motive. Most, if not all, communication is motivated by a variety of reasons. An important motive of much communication is to bring it about that the person one is addressing acquires a true belief. In 'strategic' therapy one deliberately induces a belief in the person addressed, but the truth of the belief is in itself immaterial to the communication. For the sole purpose of the communication is strategic, in the sense of being directed towards the therapeutic goal. In case it is not clear what I mean by the 'absence of a truth-centred motive' here is a simple example. Suppose I tell you that your house is on fire; my main reason for doing so is to induce you to call the fire brigade and in this way minimise the damage to your property. However, I intend to get you to do this by your acquiring the true belief that your house is on fire. My communication is 'non-strategic', since I would not have tried to encourage *you* to believe your house was burning had *I* not believed it was.

Compare this with a case where I tell you that your house is on fire to induce you to hurry home so you will be in when your children get back from school. Here my communication is 'strategic' because whether or not your house is on fire is immaterial to my reasons for telling you that it is. It might equally have served my purpose, for instance, to have told you that your house was being burgled.

It should be clear that a strategic approach is not unique to family therapy. It could, and often is used as part of an individual psychotherapy, or as part of a behaviour modification programme. On the other hand, there is nothing in the systems model as such which requires its followers to adopt a strategic approach. Nevertheless, the fact remains that the strategic approach is widely used by family therapists, some of whom regard it as essential to their work; and perhaps it is at its most effective in shaking family systems out of destructive patterns of behaviour.

Respect for people

Immanuel Kant declared the following principle to be a moral constraint on the pursuit of any goal:

> Act in such a way that you always treat humanity, whether in your person or in the person of any other, never simply as a means, but always at the same time as an end (Kant, 1785, p. 91).

The reason why we should act in this way is that human beings are rational creatures with the capacity for an autonomous will. Rationality in this sense is contrasted not with irrationality, but with non-rationality. Prawns, trees and stones are all non-rational; human beings, except perhaps for babies, morons and the comatose, are all rational, even though we are all, to a greater or lesser extent, irrational also. What is perhaps most distinctive of rational creatures is that we are able to act in pursuit of our own self-chosen goals. By this I do not mean that people can exercise choices completely in abstraction from the culture in which they live, but that we may look at the world, place our own construction (obviously derived in part from our culture) on it, and act in pursuit of our personal conception of the good. The liberal democratic tradition, certainly from Kant to the present, has taken very seriously the value of this autonomy, both as a means to the achievement of other goals, such as a relatively pleasant, pain-free existence, and also, as an end desirable in its own right, an essential ingredient of human flourishing.

As the worth of autonomy is a fundamental moral principle, its truth is incapable of demonstration, and perhaps it *needs* no proof. I shall offer none here, but would ask anyone who doubted it to consider what, if anything, is wrong with the Brave New World of Aldous Huxley's novel. My argument is aimed only at those who share my view that autonomy is essential to human dignity, and should be respected.

Identifying basic values such as autonomy and pleasure is the easy part of moral theory. It is far more difficult to figure out how the different values may work in a system which is (reasonably) consistent, plausible, and free of arbitrary principles whose sole function is to save the theory from falsification.

What is the meaning of the injunction to treat humanity never simply as a means, but always at the same time as an end? The value of a knife consists in its ability to serve as a means to the achievement of human purposes – notably cutting, spreading, or stabbing. On the other hand, people do not have a 'value' as such. We have our own purposes and projects. We are beings in virtue of which there are values. To treat someone as an end is to recognise her right to live according to her own conception of a good life. Thus making a false promise to someone in order to secure a loan which one does not intend to repay is treating her simply as a means – in this case, as a means to the satisfaction of one's own, perhaps selfish, desire. To punish someone more severely than he deserves *pour encourager les autres* is to treat him just as a means to an end – in this case, perhaps the reduction of crime in society.

There is a moral theory (classical utilitarianism), according to which the right thing to do is to act so as to produce the greatest net increase in pleasure. According to this theory, all pleasures can be compared on a single scale, so that a tiny benefit for each of a vast number of people could outweigh an enormous harm for a single individual. Thus gladiatorial contests might be justifiable on this view, provided that the population is sufficiently bloodthirsty and television coverage is sufficiently widespread. The fact that classical utilitarianism appears to have this consequence is a common reason for rejecting it.

The morality associated with the Kantian principle would rule out gladiatorial contests on two grounds. First, although it is often *rational* for an individual to forgo the satisfaction of a present desire in order to have more satisfaction later, it may not be *moral* to sacrifice all of one person's desire – satisfaction to produce a greater aggregate in society as a whole; for the individual is not in any way compensated by the increase in desire-satisfaction in society. Second, people have interests of different levels of significance. There are some things which are necessary for a person to be able to live a worthwhile life. Let us call these a person's 'vital interests'. According to the principle, it is always wrong to sacrifice anyone's *vital* interests for any gains for the non-vital interests of that person or anyone else.

One important principle of liberal democracy is that autonomy is a vital interest. Brave New World is, by the principles of classical utilitariansim, a far better society than our own. Yet we think it awful, and Huxley wrote his novel as a warning about what might happen if we are not very careful. The awfulness is not that some people's lives are made a misery in order to serve the overall good of society, but rather that the majority of the population are completely lacking in autonomy. Society has been arranged so that nearly everyone is contented in a harmonious world, with little civil strife. The cost is that people are not interested in what the world is really like, why things happen the way they do; and they have no desire to work out their own interpretation of life or arrive at their own set of values.

The citizens of Brave New World are not treated as ends in themselves, even though the behaviour of their leaders may be benevolent. They are *treated instrumentally*, their wills are manipulated; perhaps to serve the interests of the rulers, perhaps for their own 'benefit'. Thus, pleasant though Brave New World may be, its allure should be resisted because it seriously violates the Kantian principle.

Kant himself was especially concerned to answer the question 'How is morality possible at all, given the fact that human beings are by and large governed by selfish desires? He does not seem sensitive to the existence of genuine moral dilemmas, and proposes as a test for the acceptability of any moral principle, that its adherents be able to will that the principle become a universal law; in other words that it be a principle acceptable not just to the person following it, but to any other rational creature, including its 'victim'. Thus, on a strict interpretation, it seems that one should always respect the interests, and in particular, the autonomy of *all* parties with whom one has dealings. One should never lie to, steal from, cheat, manipulate, or harm anyone, ever, since the principle which justified the behaviour could not be accepted by its 'victim', and therefore could not be 'willed to be a universal law' in the appropriate sense.

One way in which psychotherapy differs from some more conventional forms of psychiatry is that the former takes seriously the human need for autonomy, and something like a Kantian principle of respect for people.

Interpreted in this strict way, the Kantian principle is obviously inconsistent with strategic therapy, since the latter requires a degree of manipulation, and certainly something far short of candour. However, the encounter between the strategic approach and the principle of respect for people need not be so brief; for the principle interpreted in this way is implausible – and not just because so construed it is inconsistent with the practices of zealous family therapists.

Many conflicts of interests within the world are merely apparent, and can be resolved satisfactorily by rational debate and the provision of new information. However, some conflicts are genuine, in the sense that one person's gain really is the other's loss. Sometimes even vital interests conflict. In such circumstances it may be impossible to avoid harming at least one of the parties. Doing nothing may harm both. What the 'strict' Kantian principle would prescribe in such circumstances, I do not know. Unless it appeals to the dubious claim that it is impossible to harm someone by not performing a required action, the strict principle leads to the conclusion that in these circumstances one cannot avoid acting wrongly. This counsel of despair is of no use to a deliberating agent, and should, I think, be rejected, though now is not the time to spell out the argument for the rejection. More plausible is the 'liberal' interpretation which requires one to treat respect for people as a desirable goal. For a similar interpretation, in a different context, see Graham (1982). Whilst recognising that autonomy has value independent of its contribution to a pleasant life, one realises that there may be occasions when it is impossible to avoid the violation of someone's autonomy. In these circumstances, the principle prescribes that one acts so as to best promote the *goal* of autonomy.

Just as there may be inter-personal conflicts of interest, so there may be inter-temporal conflicts within a person. We exist through time, and what may accord with, so to speak, my present interests, may conflict with my long-term interests. In such cases what does the principle of respect for people prescribe? Or proscribe? At the theoretical level, I think it would prescribe that one acted to promote the person's long-term interests. However, this is not at all the same thing as to say that one should act always with the person's long-term interests consciously in mind. Some goals are best pursued indirectly, as family therapists writing about cures for impotence are the first to recognise. Among the general justifying aims of therapy is, I suppose, an increase in the autonomy of those in therapy.

A key question for family therapists is, therefore, whether the value of respect for people, including respect for their autonomy, is better promoted by using indirect or devious strategies when it seems appropriate, than by adopting a convention whereby they are avoided except in very extreme circumstances.

I shall consider two major sources of possible moral dilemma for strategic family therapists. One concerns the fact that people other than the identified patient may be brought into the therapeutic process either unwillingly, or unwittingly. In this sense, it could be said that they are being used as a means to the achievement of the therapist's goal. Second, much use of strategies within therapy certainly appears to be manipulative of the people at whom the therapy is directed; and it seems to be important to its success that the targets of therapy remain ignorant of the therapist's beliefs and immediate intentions. Strategic therapy appears to be dishonest, and being dishonest to someone is one way of failing to respect her or him.

Roping in the family

A typical problem of the first type might occur if an adolescent with behavioural problems has been designated in need of therapy. Suppose he has been scapegoated by his family, and, in the opinion of the therapist, his problems could best be solved by treating the whole family including his mother and father, who fail to recognise that there is anything wrong with the family, except for the awful behaviour of their son 'In spite of all we've done for him'. Let us suppose that there is no principled moral objection to persuading the parents to participate in family therapy by informing them of your actual opinion that such a therapy offers the best chances for the boy's recovery. If it would work, I am sure most would agree that such an approach would be desirable. But precisely this sort of parent may well not believe you, and maybe entirely unpersuaded by a direct approach. Furthermore, if you told them the truth, that the family system was not working properly, and that they would have to change in order to make it do so, they might run a mile. So, the best way of persuading them to join the therapy would be to manipulate them in some way. This could be either by failing to reveal the purpose of having an interview with the whole family, or possibly by threatening them in some way. 'Unless you do come, we shall have to do so and so ...' (knowing that they could not accept so and so). This might be said, even though the therapist would actually have the authority to decide whether or not 'so and so' was actually done. The decision may not be out of his hands.

To simplify, I shall assume that the therapist rationally believes that to involve other members of the family offers the best chance of helping the identified patient, and that this is why he considers such a policy. There are two main cases to consider. The first is where the family is locked into a destructive cycle of behaviour which harms all of them. It is assumed that the therapy will jolt the system into changing in a way which will benefit all the family. The other case is where there is a direct conflict of interest between the identified patient and one or more members of the family.

An example of the former is described by Cade (1979). A couple had not been out together for 15 years, and they blamed this on their now 16-year-old son, who was described as 'violent, destructive, and an incessant bully towards his younger siblings'. He had been labelled 'schizoid' and 'psychopathic' by various 'professionals' in the past. Instead of just offering yet another supposed solution to the child's problems, the therapist involved the parents, by asking them to discuss where they would like to go out together, were they only able to do so. The parents and the children were warned that it might be inadvisable for the parents to go out on account of their 16-year-old's unpredictable behaviour.

> At the next session, the mother triumphantly reported an enjoyable trip she and her husband had made to a local theatre. The children had posed no problems at all; the 16-year-old had even prepared a hot drink on their return. They were planning a further outing later that week. I expressed guarded pleasure but cautioned continued wariness, repeating much of what I had said in the previous session (Cade, 1979, p. 100).

It is clear that the intervention here benefits, and was reasonably expected to benefit, the whole family, since they are locked into a pattern of behaviour which undermines the autonomy of all of them. Here is an inter-temporal conflict of autonomy interests for the parents. The long-term autonomy of the parents is in fact promoted by the intervention. Even if they had to be brought into therapy surreptitiously, I cannot see that the pursuit of such a policy by the therapist is inconsistent with the principle of respect for people, under its 'liberal' interpretation.

The other sort of case is perhaps more problematic. Suppose a housewife is identified as depressed, of low self-esteem, and generally unable to stand on her own two feet. The therapist believes that her problems stem from an unsatisfactory relationship with her husband. He is unsupportive of her, offers little help or encouragement with the children, expects to be waited on hand and foot when he comes home from work, and always sees that the demands of his work are given top priority in the household. In fact the relationship is unequal, and the husband is benefiting greatly from the acceptance by his wife of the status quo, which is damaging her. Her 'cure' lies in a changed understanding on her *and* her husband's part, of what it is reasonable to expect from a marriage partner. To bring the husband into therapy may work against his interests, and the therapist may believe that it will.

When, as in this case, there is a direct conflict of interests, I think the therapist should make appeal to the 'liberal' interpretation of the principle of respect. In this situation it is impossible unequivocally to respect the autonomy of each party. A failure to bring in the husband is violation of respect for the autonomy of the wife no less than inveigling him into therapy may be a violation of respect for his. If the autonomy interests of the two parties cancel each other out, then decisions should rest on other considerations, such as justice and utility. In such a case it is likely that both will tend to be on the side of the wife.

Strategy and paradox

Nowhere is a family therapist more vulnerable to the charge of violating the principle of respect for people than in the adoption of a strategic approach, and the most common strategic weapon is paradox. So it is to the use of paradox that I address this section. Cade (1979) writes the following:

> I never explain the way in which a paradox works to an individual or a family even after its use has produced a desired change. Understanding or insight is not seen as a prerequisite for change nor necessary during or after change. It is of concern to many professionals that such a use of paradox involves 'trickery' which is 'manipulative' and lacking in sincerity (p. 104).

He answers the implied moral criticism by quoting with approval an argument from Watzlawick *et al.*, which is also criticised by Collier (chapter 8):

> Sincerity has lately become a catchword, a hypocrisy in its own right, associated in a murky way with the idea that there is such a thing as a right

view of the world – usually one's own view. It also seems associated with the idea that manipulation is not only bad, but can be avoided. Nobody, unfortunately, has ever explained how this can be done. It is difficult to imagine how any behaviour in the presence of another person can avoid being a communication of one's own view of the nature of one's relationship with that person and how it can, therefore, fail to influence that person . . . . The problem, therefore, is not how influence and manipulation can be avoided, but how they can best be comprehended and used in the interest of the patient (1974, p. xv).

The argument is, to say the least, uncompelling. In particular the claim that 'manipulation' is unavoidable is not made out at all. The argument runs as follows:

1   It is difficult to imagine how any behaviour in the presence of another person can avoid being a communication of one's own view of the nature of one's relationship with that person.
2   Therefore it is difficult to imagine how any behaviour in the presence of another person can fail to influence that person.
3   Therefore the problem is not how influence and manipulation can be avoided, but how they can best be comprehended and used in the interest of the patient.

Premise (1) is doubtful, since much behaviour seems successfully to conceal an agent's view of the nature of his relationship with a person in his presence.

If, however, we grant (1), (2) I think, becomes plausible, even though it is not entailed by (1). In fact (2) is plausible, even without (1), since trivially, any perception has *some* influence on the perceiver.

(3) certainly does not follow from (2) since manipulation is referred to neither in premise (1) nor in (2). It would be plausible to accept (3) on the strength of (2) only if one assumes that 'influence' and 'manipulation' are synonymous. But they are not. For 'influence', in the sense which makes (2) plausible, may be entirely unintentional, and not goal-directed. On the other hand 'manipulation', certainly as practised by strategic therapists, *is* intentional and goal-directed. Second, even if one restricts 'influence' only to 'intentional and goal-directed influence', it is not the same thing as 'manipulation'. I may (successfully) influence you by sincerely voicing my opinion on a subject, without recourse to manipulation.

Philosophy, and I daresay the theory of psychotherapy, are littered with bad arguments for sound conclusions. I do not think that Watzlawick *et al.*, above, is a case in point, although it certainly does contain a bad argument. Even though it is impossible for a therapist to have no influence over her patients, the sort of manipulation practised in strategic therapy could in principle be avoided, since it is predicated on a decision by the therapist deliberately to create a false impression, usually about the beliefs and expectations of the therapist. Of course, it may be that communication complexities are such that it is impossible to prevent all misunderstandings between therapist and patients; but a therapist *could* rationally strive to keep such false impressions to a minimum.

I therefore reject this blanket justification for strategic therapy. On the other hand, a total rejection of 'strategy' is equally unwarranted. It seems that strategic therapy covers a vast range of interventions, some of which violate nobody's autonomy, others of which do so in an unacceptable way, and an interesting category in the middle. Let us consider some of the uses of paradox discussed by Cade (1979).

First, a man sought help, having found it increasingly difficult to maintain an erection. The therapist saw this man and his girlfriend, told the man he should learn to control the behaviour of his penis more effectively, and with this in view, he was instructed to try to prevent his penis from becoming or staying erect, in spite of his lover's strenuous efforts to excite him. He failed, and the intervention succeeded.

In this case any manipulation by the therapist is incidental, since deception is not essential to the therapy. It is well known that one of the causes of chronic impotence is anxiety in anticipation of possible failure to get or maintain an erection. Trying not to get an erection may remove the source of anxiety. If the patient fails to get an erection he has successfully carried out his prescribed task. If he does get an erection, he has succeeded in an area where past failure had led him into therapy in the first place. This is a good strategy for reducing the anxiety which is the likely cause of his continuing impotence; for he is bound to succeed and so has nothing to be anxious about. The insomniac, who was asked to perform complicated, boring tasks at irregular intervals through the night, is a similar case. Although the therapy consists of a 'paradoxical' instruction, duplicity is not intrinsic to it. There is no principled reason why the man with sexual difficulties and the insomniac could not think up and adopt the paradoxical solutions for themselves.

A second type of case is where, although what the therapist says is literally false, no deception takes place. Cade's example of the woman who had been defined as 'inadequate' and 'chronically depressed' seems to be an interesting case of paradoxical command of the only-superficially-deceptive-type. The woman rarely got out of bed before noon; her house was in a terrible mess; her husband, whom she continually berated for his laziness, stayed home to look after the house; she did little cooking or housework, and spent most of the day lying on a settee in a housecoat.

Cade, the therapist,

... expressed considerable concern over her state of health, saying that I was extremely worried about her. I expressed shock at how early she was attempting to get up each day for a woman in her condition. Under no circumstances should she be up before at least three o'clock in the afternoon; if necessary she should stay in bed all day. As for cooking and housework, these were to be done by the rest of the family; the woman was solemnly warned that she was not to attempt such tasks ... (1979, p. 91).

The result of this intervention was that the woman got up the next morning at 8.30, to make the breakfast.

She tidied the house from top to bottom, then took the children down to the shops to buy toys, decorations, and the Christmas foodstuffs ... On my next visit the family reported that it had been the best Christmas they had had for years (p. 92).

A paradoxical command here was disobeyed by the woman, and it is clear that this was the intention of the therapist. This excellent intervention was perhaps the best possible way of pointing out to the woman the absurdity of her position – by taking it to its logical conclusion. I think the absurdity *was* conveyed to the woman, and she was then able to help herself. The strategy of the therapist is similar to that of inviting someone to see a play which one hopes will reveal a truth to the person about her own life. Works of fiction are literally false, but they are not deceptive, because authors do not intend their audiences to take them literally. Communication takes place at different levels, and some paradoxical interventions, although false at a superficial level, are true at a deeper level. This sort of strategy is very close to the use of metaphor (see Cade, 1979, p. 102).

There are many contexts where the message communicated differs from the literal meaning of the sentences used in the communication. Consider, for example, J. L. Austin's famous example of the undergraduate's end-of-term philosophy report which simply said 'His handwriting is excellent and his English is grammatical'. Sometimes, speaking the literal truth may create a false impression – this may be especially likely in the context of therapy. Under these conditions the goal of honesty might sometimes dictate literal dishonesty.

Another strategy is relabelling. Consider the following example from Weakland *et al.* (1974):

Redefining behaviour labelled hostile as concerned interest, for example, may be therapeutically useful whether or not either label is true, and that such truth can never be firmly established. All that is observable is that some labels provoke difficulties, whilst others, achievable by redefinition, promote adjustment and harmony ... (p.156).

In these cases there appears to be deception, but this is supposedly off-set by the possibility either that there are no correct labels, or that at least it is impossible to have enough evidence rationally to arrive at a belief that one particular label is nearer the truth than a rival. Nevertheless, the deception is genuine. Honesty would, perhaps, require the therapist to *say* that these labels are bandied about in the absence of adequate evidence. He could then continue 'I think it is more useful to regard your behaviour as if it expressed concerned interest'. This would avoid morally unsatisfactory deviousness. Whether such honesty would destroy the therapeutic effectiveness is, of course another matter.

Finally, there is full-blown deception. This is the most worrying form of strategic intervention, since it seems to violate directly the principle of respect for people. Amongst strategies which use genuine deception is one described by Papp (1983) where the therapist retires to consult with colleagues behind the screen, and then returns ostensibly carrying a message from the other members of the team, perhaps to the effect that they are worried about the therapist. No ambiguity is present here. A lie is told deliberately, in order to produce a therapeutic effect. It is not possible to justify this sort of intervention by claiming that there is no genuine truth of the matter; or by appeal to different levels of meaning; or by claiming that there is no strictly avoidable manipulation. I refer the reader to Collier's chapter in this volume for an extended discussion of truth and reality.

Full-blown deception does harm its victim, even if the victim is unaware of its having taken place. What makes the discovery of deception painful is the awfulness of deception. It is not that deception is awful simply because its discovery is painful. I may be harmed by malicious gossip behind my back which destroys my reputation, even though I never discover my reputation has been destroyed; nor suffer materially as a result. See Nagel (1979) for an interesting discussion of painless harm.

Nevertheless, it does not follow that deceptive strategic therapy is always immoral. If, as is apparently sometimes the case, this sort of deception is the only way of preventing worse harm befalling its targets, then it may well be justified. However, one should regard it as bad in itself, and always requiring a specific justification.

I am grateful to Adam Morton for pointing out in discussion that in order for this analysis to be helpful some account must be offered of how the gravity of painless harm is to be measured. All deception is in itself harmful, because it is an attack upon the autonomy of the person deceived. However, some deceptions are far worse than others, and not just because they are more painful. Suppose a colleague has just had a new hair-do. He asks you what you think of it. Even if you thought it was awful, respect for the colleague might induce you to say, at the very least, that it was all right. On this occasion, the harm of the deception is trivial, compared to the harm which could by done by candour. Candour would certainly be painful for the colleague, and pain is bad. On the other hand, consider a long-term deceptive adulterous relationship. The deception here may be very harmful, as would be evidenced by the strength of feeling which its discovery would engender. The deception threatens the original relationship in a more insidious way than the adultery itself. How might one begin to estimate the relative harm of different deceptive therapeutic strategies?

I think the key to this is to be found in the deceived person's desires. What makes deceptive adultery wrong is primarily the fact that the deceived person wants very much not to be deceived. Some couples live in 'open' relationships where it is agreed that each partner may have sexual relationships outside the couple. Sometimes they agree not to discuss each other's 'outside' encounters. They could go a stage further, and agree that each will keep these affairs a secret from the other. Here it is unlikely that the couple would mind very much if their partner was deceptive about an affair. Deception on this issue in this case would, accordingly, be less harmful than in the more common situation.

The relationship between desire satisfaction and autonomy is complex and requires a paper (at least) to itself (see Lindley, 1986). However, we can say that deceptive strategic therapy harms its 'beneficiary' directly, in proportion to the importance to the deceived of the desires it frustrates. Thus, one may speculate that probably no serious harm is done in cases where the therapist deceptively reports that a colleague behind the screen is concerned about the state of the therapist, and that an end to the session is recommended. Truth about this matter may be far from the centre of the client's concerns. Compare this, however, with another of Cade's cases – that of a single mother and her young child, who were referred for therapy.

> She was described as being of 'low self-esteem', was grossly overweight, dressed shabbily and her hair was generally unkempt. Her house was ill kept, the walls dirty and she rarely went out except to her part-time office cleaning job. She had had no contact with her parents for some considerable time and felt that they had rejected her. Her son, five years of age, was failing to achieve what his school considered to be his potential. She had received supportive therapy over a considerable period of time with no significant change (1979, p. 101).

Here the therapist had already agreed, prior to the first interview, to a strategy in which whenever the woman 'put herself down' the therapist would criticise her a bit more, irrespective of whether the therapist thought the criticism justifiable.

When the woman talked about her unwillingness to go out the therapist agreed that it must be hard to go out without feeling people were looking at her; for she was so large. The woman reacted angrily to this, saying that:

> ... it was the therapist's job to listen not to agree. The therapist nodded in a concerned manner then advised the woman that the one thing she could depend on was that the therapist would be completely honest with her (1979, p. 101).

What is disturbing about this case is that the woman clearly is someone who placed great store on honesty about her physical and psychological condition. This deception was a more serious violation of her autonomy. Imagine how she would react to the discovery that the therapist had been deceiving her all along. The therapeutic goal has been achieved, but at a considerable cost – the thwarting of a desire or set of desires which are very important to the beneficiary of the therapy. It is true that 'he who wills the end wills the means'. But the end of the 'patient' may be not just to become able to cope adequately with life, but to learn to cope whilst not being manipulated or deceived in respect of crucial desires.

In conclusion I would say that those who expect philosophy to offer a neat solution to the moral problems attending family therapy will be disappointed. The principal opponents of manipulative intervention as such rest their case either on unacceptable principles or false premises. On the other hand, those who fail to recognise the existence of moral problems in this area are also the victims of sophistry or confusion.

It is, I think, a practical inevitability that even morally principled therapists will sometimes have to use deceptive strategies. However, this should not be a ground for complacency. What emerges from a study of the use of paradox and other strategic techniques by therapists is that they must be very gratifying techniques to practise. The therapist wields considerable power over patients, and the results are often startlingly dramatic.

Simply because this is the case, there is a danger that therapists may be seduced by the attractions of a swift deceptive strategy, into treating a client with contempt. Because of this danger, and the fact that deception is anyway harmful in its own right, an ethical code for therapists should include a strong presumption against deception. Full-blown deceptive strategies, especially where the deception is over a matter of great concern to the client, should be used only as a last resort and in exceptional circumstances.

8

THE LANGUAGE OF OBJECTIVITY
AND THE ETHICS OF REFRAMING

Andrew Collier

My aim in this paper is to reply to and, I hope, to refute the following claims made in Watzlawick, Weakland and Fisch (1974) and quoted by Brian Cade (Walrond-Skinner, 1979, p. 104):

> 'Sincerity' has lately become a catchword, a hypocrisy in its own right, associated in a murky way with the idea that there is such a thing as a 'right' view of the world – usually one's own view.

I shall argue that a view would not be 'one's own' if one did not believe it to be the right view – which of course does not mean one would not reconsider it if given grounds for doing so; that there is in principle a right way of viewing the world, to which we may have more or less close approximations; and that the value of sincerity is indeed based on this in a perfectly clear and unmurky way. The quoted passage continues:

> It also seems associated with the idea that 'manipulation' is not only bad, but can be avoided. Nobody, unfortunately, has ever explained how this can be done (p. 104).

I also want to argue that, other things being equal, manipulation is bad, and that it is easy to see that it can often be avoided. Where possible I will relate my points to the therapeutic situations described by Brian Cade. I do not in fact think that all the strategies described involve manipulation or insincerity, and where they do, it may be possible to defend them despite these failings, because of the relief of suffering achieved. Nevertheless, I think that these failings are *prima facie* undesirable, and should be avoided where an alternative therapeutic strategy is available; and that the attempt to forestall criticism of them by discarding the aim of objectivity has far more far-reaching harmful effects.

First, the most 'philosophical' of the issues involved: *realism*, the idea that the world is as it is independently of our opinions about it. Brian Cade's view that 'reality is what we choose to define it as' is clearly opposed to this. Now, attacks on realism may claim general applicability, but in fact they are always selective. Nobody really doubts the objectivity of statements like 'the potatoes are on the kitchen table' or 'Bristol is further west than London'. Most often the area selected for a non-realist account is one with which the non-realist in question has no practical involvement: the non-realist account of physical illness espoused by the Christian Science movement is unlikely to convince a surgeon.

Non-realist accounts are sometimes given of the more abstract parts of the sciences. This is the main site of philosophical controversy about realism. I regard the sort of argument given by Roy Bhaskar as conclusive on this issue – argument to the effect that we can only make sense of the role of experiment in science on realist assumptions (Bhaskar, 1978). But this is a different issue since there are no genuine experiments in the social sciences[1]. So I shall only suggest that it is the *strangeness* of scientific accounts compared with everyday discourse that makes non-realist interpretations of them so widely credible. We are not tempted by non-realist accounts of matters we can test in practice.

The other area in which non-realism is a serious temptation is human and social reality. Here the problem is the great diversity of opinions and difficulty, often the impossibility, of discovering which is true. This impossibility does not entitle us to regard none (or all) as true. Take the claim that all human societies passed through a stage of matriarchy. The evidence on this issue, which has long divided the experts, is inconclusive, and it is unlikely that decisive new evidence will be turned up. Yet the claim must be true or false, and which it is does not depend on us. There are people who would very much like it to be true (or false) since it is thought to have bearing on the prospects of feminism. Yet it is impossible to *choose* to believe it (or disbelieve it). Someone who claimed to do so would in fact be *pretending* to believe it. For to believe that something is true is to hold that that is how it is whatever anyone thinks of it.

As a result of the notorious complexity of human realities, any description of them, even if true in itself, will be incomplete in ways that might be considered important. It will often be necessary to criticise such a description, not as false but as one-sided. This ought to be obvious, but much of the polemic against objectivity gains such plausibility and attractiveness as it has from presenting objective description as one-sided, schematic description, while many-sided, complex description is seen as inevitably non-objective. Thus Brian Cade and Philippa Seligman contrast the idea of belief-systems as absolute 'realities' with the view that they are 'ways of organising potentially limitless, sometimes incomprehensible, data into some graspable framework which can *never* be right or wrong but only more or less useful' (Cade and Seligman, 1981).

Three distinctions are being superimposed here: between dogmatically held beliefs and those that are open to revision; between schematic and fuller conceptions; and between the ideas that beliefs can be discoveries about reality, and that they are imposed on it for reasons of utility. Clearly dogmatism and schematism or one-sidedness are to be avoided, but that in no way commits us to treating beliefs as useful fictions.

This point about dogmatism needs stressing. A dogmatist is someone whose beliefs are not up for revision in the light of new evidence. It is a common misconception that to regard one's beliefs as objectively true is to be unwilling to consider new evidence. In fact, it is to expect that that new evidence will not lead to their revision, but it is also to recognise the relevance of evidence. If beliefs are meant to be objectively true, they must be open to refutation by new evidence, and it is clear what the relevance of the new evidence will be, i.e. it may show that, in fact, things are different. If beliefs are something other than truth claims, it is no longer clear why anyone should look at the evidence against them; hence to remove the objective reference of belief is to license dogmatism, not to avoid it. Indeed it is doubtful whether, religious fundamentalism aside, there have ever existed dogmatic claims to objective truth; the typical dogmatist does not care about objective truth, because their beliefs have other determinants (and even religious fundamentalism can take the form of Tertullian's 'I believe because it is absurd'). In this respect, it seems to me that the repudiation of claims to objectivity in Brian Cade's paper is a typically dogmatic move: it means that if someone comes along and says 'but the facts are different', he can reply 'so much the worse for the facts', or rather, simply 'I see no facts'.

The whole concept of 'reframing' as set forth in that article remains ambiguous between making a differently selective description of some situation, and imposing a different viewpoint, justified as nicer to believe rather than as fuller or more accurate. Thus after starting with the bald assertion that 'reality is what we choose to define it as', we later read that the new frame must fit the facts as well as or better than the one it replaces, though 'facts' is given scare quotes.

I think there is another idea underlying this concept of reframing. This is the idea that to describe a situation is *ipso facto* to change it, so that there is no situation independent of the description, against which the description could be measured for truth or falsehood. Now it is clear that the possession of a description of a situation by someone involved in that situation makes a difference.

But (i) the difference is made, not by the simple fact that the situation has been described in such-and-such a way, but precisely by the *possession* of that description by someone *involved* in the situation; (ii) it may be that the alteration brought about by the participant's new belief makes that belief false, even though it was true before. In the simplest case, suppose Jack comes to accept the description 'Jack was misinterpreting Jill's behaviour as aggressive', then he will no longer be misinterpreting it in that way. But this does not generate a paradox, since the misunderstanding was at one time, the acceptance of the description at another. (iii) in order to understand how describing a situation can change it, we have to recognise that the simple fact of a description existing does *not* change it; for unless the description is one thing and the situation described another, we cannot say what the situation was before it was changed. Again, a changed description does not by itself change the situation, for if it did, we could not give any sense to the idea that it was a *changed* description of *one* situation.

The confusion of the situation with description generates a paradox rather like the Gilbertian one at the end of *The Mikado*:

> When your Majesty says, 'Let a thing be done,' it's as good as done – practically, it *is* done – because your Majesty's will is law. Your Majesty says, 'Kill a gentleman,' and a gentleman is told off to be killed. Consequently that gentleman is as good as dead – practically, he *is* dead – and if he is dead, why not say so? (W. S. Gilbert, 1876, p. 54)

(iv) The acceptance of a description of a situation by its participants will alter that situation in exactly the same way *whether it is true or false*. But to give out a false description in order to alter the situation is manipulative in the sense discussed below. The confusion of change in description with change in situation could be used as an alibi for such manipulation.

There is of course the special case in which acceptance of a description at one time brings it about that that description is true at a later time. But this *is* a special case, and whatever special ethical principles apply to it cannot be generalised to other cases.

Finally, I would suggest that the frequent use in social work literature of the word 'define' where common English usage requires the word 'describe' (as in 'Mrs Jones was defined as lazy'), is not just an innocent piece of jargon, but eases the path of the mistaken idea that to describe is to transform.

The ethics of language use

The language of beliefs, i.e. claims about what is true of the real world, and fact-stating language generally, is by no means the only language game available to us. There are forms of language for supposing, advising, evaluating, etc. which can be used to communicate other things than objective facts, and in some of the cases discussed by Brian Cade as uses of paradoxical strategies, that is what is going on. But in some cases the language used by the therapists is the language of objectivity: it plays the game of giving information, contradicting incompatible accounts of the facts, and so on. It is where this fact-like language is used, while objectivity is disavowed (disavowed in the paper, that is, not to the clients, to whom the appearance of objectivity is sustained throughout) that the charge of insincerity can be levelled. The case described by Brian Cade, in which it was given out that a member of the team had become emotionally disturbed by what the patient was saying, falls into this category. For the question whether such a thing had occurred is as straightforwardly factual as the question whether the potatoes are on the table or under the sink.

The majority of the 'paradoxical injunctions' referred to, however, are not like this at all, for the most part, because they are injunctions, not statements. Telling someone to do something in the expectation that the outcome of the attempt will be to achieve some quite different result[2] is not to tell a lie or to express feelings or opinions that one does not have. Other cases again could be seen as the use of heavy irony rather than paradox,[3] somewhat in the tradition of the Spartan authorities referred to by Rousseau:

Certain drunkards from Samos polluted the tribunal of the Ephors: the next day, a public edict gave Samians the permission to be filthy (Rousseau, 1966, p. 106).

Brian Cade stresses that the new light in which patients are induced to see their situations is usually more favourable. In the limit case, this may just be a matter of using commending rather than condemning language. But usually, words commend or condemn by virtue of their descriptive meaning, not independently of it. Hence to 'reframe' is to redescribe, not merely to re-evaluate. Thus in the final case he mentions, where the possessive, authoritarian father is told what a concerned, responsible father he is, this is neither a lie, nor a mere euphemism. Possessiveness may well be an expression of deep concern, just as wife-beating may be an expression of passionate love. But it is obviously not the only possible such expression, and not a good one. No doubt the half-truth told to this father may mollify him and open him to persuasion about the other half of the truth. That is the right use of tact. But it is important to be clear firstly that what is said is true, even if not the whole truth; then that his being persuaded of the other part of the truth – that the way he shows his concern is open to improvement – is the aim, even if this is not done verbally. Tact here means inserting the wedge of truth thin end first. But if concern for truth is simply left out, tact becomes something different: as it has been cynically defined, 'saying "nice doggie" till you can find a rock'.

This question of the implications of the type of language used (both in the therapeutic situation and in the case notes) is in a sense the central question of this paper, so let me enumerate my main points:

1. That there are uses of language which do not make claims about what is the case in the world independently of our knowledge of it, and uses which do; many of the sentences in Brian Cade's case reports fall into the latter category – both statements made to clients, and reports and theoretical explanations in the paper.
2. That the choice of this type of language commits the user to claiming truth and objectivity for his account of the world, and hence to recognising that he might be mistaken, that an incompatible account might be true, and if so, that his own must be false.
3. That to use language in this apparently objective way and then deny in one's second-order discourse,[4] that any account can be objectively true, is to rob the original discourse of any content: if a neighbour comes in and says 'Your goat has got into my garden and is eating my magnolias – but nothing I say has any relation to any reality independent of my thoughts' – one would be none the wiser about the activities of one's goat.
4. That a lot of the first-order accounts not only use an objectivity-claiming type of language, but could not be translated into or substituted by a discourse that did not. So am I not just claiming that Brian Cade talks as if he did not take his second-order theories seriously, but that if he did take them seriously, he would have to stop talking altogether about most of the matters concerned.

We are left with the more moderate interpretation: that different accounts may both (or all) be true, but may select different aspects of the situation. On this interpretation, 'reframing' becomes simply recommending that attention be paid to other aspects of the situation than it had.

It might possibly be objected here that one such selective presentation of the facts may indeed be incompatible with another, without either being false, in the way that the two pictures in a Gestalt switch drawing cannot be perceived together. It is worth saying as a caution about this much-worn analogy that such drawings have to be very carefully constructed: a slight slip and they will only appear one way. I mention this to throw doubt on the common assumption that everything can be seen more than one way.

The central point though, is that although one can't *see* the two pictures simultaneously, there is no difficulty about giving an objective description. This could be done either in the neutral terms of geometry, or more to the point, by saying: 'it looks like a duck if you focus one way, and a rabbit if you focus the other', or whatever. Likewise we can say things like 'he loves his daughter very much, but his possessiveness stifles her', or, as I once read in an anthropology book, 'Australian Aboriginal women are very good, caring mothers, but sometimes cook their babies for supper'.

If we are unable to keep both aspects of the picture in mind at once, that is due to the limits of the imagination. The paradoxical description does not contain logically contradictory statements – both parts can be true. It describes different and dissonant but equally real aspects of those notoriously paradoxical creatures, people. We need to be imaginative enough to be open to such paradoxical descriptions, but that does not commit us to treating incompatible statements as both true.

Insofar as therapy works by means of language, the ethics of language use is also the ethics of therapy. This brings us to the question of manipulation. I doubt if any critic of manipulation has thought that just any way of affecting other people's behaviour is manipulative. Examples of manipulative behaviours would be: cajoling, flattering insincerely, lying, expressing unfelt emotions, moral blackmail, etc. To communicate one's own view of the situation (verbally or non-verbally) is not to manipulate; it is to let the other person know what one thinks or feels, and hence increase their possibilities of effective action. Manipulation occurs when a person's actions are controlled by getting them to misunderstand the situation. The value which is violated in manipulation is a *cognitive* value, which might be called 'autonomy', but only on condition that the notion is not interpreted as independence of other people, self-sufficiency or impassibility, which are dangerous illusions. Autonomy here means the power to base one's actions on a reasonable awareness of oneself and others and the world around. Autonomy in this sense is surely an important index of health; anyway, it is something that most people value, and value for itself, not only as a means to other values such as freedom from pain, or integration into a harmonious set of relationships. The harm involved in violation of someone's autonomy is not merely either the deception or consequences of it adverse to their interests, but that the agent is compromised in their actions by a false belief about something close to their heart.

I am not claiming that autonomy is an absolute value in the sense that it overrides all others. But it is a value, and there is therefore a *prima facie* presumption against manipulative therapies, in that they violate it.

Different medical therapies stand in different relations to autonomy. Purely physiological methods operate independently of the patient's awareness of what is happening to them, but the good doctor will still recognise the patient's autonomy to the extent of telling them the nature of the disease and cure. Psychoanalysis and certain group therapies approximating to it claim to operate in a manner to which the patient's self-awareness is an essential element; insofar as they live up to their claims, they are essentially autonomy enhancing.

Placebos, etc., the effectiveness of which depends on *lack* of true understanding by the patient, can quite justifiably be called manipulative; the onus is on their practitioners to show in each case that such a therapy is acceptable.

Systems and their transformation

Finally a few words about the way in which the foregoing discussion ties up with the systems theory which has been a common assumption of much discussion about family therapy. I have no intention of going into theoretical details about the nature of systems: it is possible to leave this concept at a fairly untheorised level for the present purpose.[5]

I suspect that behind the idea that objective truth has no application in the context of family systems is the idea that systems – unlike some other things – do not exist in the real world, but are imposed on it by us. There might then be objectively true answers to questions about houses, dogs, cats, people – but not about families, societies, cultures, economies: in a word, not about systems. Systems would then be seen as more or less arbitrary groupings of 'real' things – in the present case, of people.

In disputing this view, let me first suggest that it cannot be consistently applied, because people are, in fact, themselves systems – particular, complex organisations of living cells (which are, in turn, systems of molecules, which are systems of atoms, and so on). Indeed, all the things of which we know are systems, so if systems are not real, nothing is.

Suppose it is said that any systems larger than human individuals are unreal: families, political and economic formations, and so on. I would reply that they are only too damn real, as anyone who seriously tries to alter them will find out. They will not be altered simply by changing our attitude to them, by 'reframing'. This is the point at which an apparently academic and metaphysical issue – idealism versus realism – has practical effects of the first importance. For if systems are real, and can only be changed by a serious struggle based on a realistic assessment of them, then any attempt to eliminate their unacceptable features by changing people's attitudes to them in an optimistic direction can only help to preserve intact their real unacceptable features. It is the age-old alternative to changing the world: re-interpreting it. In political contexts, this is the essence of all conservative ideology. It is *idealism* in the precise sense that Marx gave to that word – illustrated by the little parable which concludes the preface to *The German Ideology* (1845):

Once upon a time a valiant fellow had the idea that men were drowned in water only because they were possessed with the idea of gravity. If they were to knock this notion out of their heads, say by stating it to be a superstition, a religious concept, they would be sublimely proof against any danger from water. His whole life long he fought against the illusion of gravity, of whose harmful results all statistics brough him new and manifold evidence. This honest fellow was the type of the new revolutionary philosophers in Germany.

This may be illustrated by the example of industrial relations. In the view of the centre of the political spectrum in this country, industrial strife is the result of misunderstanding or individual shortsightedness, and there is a common interest between 'both sides of industry', which all reasonable people should promote. According to the Marxist view, on the other hand, strife is inevitable so long as capitalism exists; the capitalists' living is derived from the exploitation of the workers, and any reasonable worker will be a militant, pushing union demands as far as they will go. Certainly, both these 'ways of seeing things' pick out real aspects of the situation and leave out others. But to claim that they are *just* 'ways of seeing things', neither more true than the other, is to decide the issue against the Marxist, for no reasonable person would choose strife if peace and prosperity for all could be had with the aid of a bit of reframing. The Marxist account must claim greater objective truth if it is to enter the ring at all. And if it *is* true (as I believe it is) then the relativist account can only serve as a piece of fraud to keep the workers exploited.

I am not urging that family problems be understood on the model of class struggle, but it cannot be ruled out that there will be cases in which anyone who values human freedom will have to bring not peace but a sword, to divide the family, not unite it. The belief that all conflicts can be reframed away could inhibit this.

Certainly, there is more room for flexibility in family therapy than in class politics. Idealism may be the opium of the people, but there are legitimate medical uses for opium. Some of the successes reported in Brian Cade's papers are impressive enough to justify the techniques used, even when they are 'manipulative'. My case so far as therapeutic ethics is concerned, then, is not against such uses, which in individual cases can be justified, but against the generalised defence of them by obliterating distinctions between truth and fiction, sincerity and dissimulaton, autonomy-enhancing and manipulative treatment.

9

FAMILY THERAPY, POWER, AND RESPONSIBILITY FOR CHANGE

Philip Kingston

Use of the term 'family therapy' implies a number of assumptions which, if they remain implicit, can lead to a serious misuse of the families who experience this method. My concerns about the term are related first of all to the word 'therapy'. 'Therapy' implies pathology, and the entity which is pathological is now 'the family' instead of 'the individual'. It is interesting to compare someone going into a family to solve a problem with someone going into an industrial or commercial organisation for the same purpose. We call the former 'family therapy' but we do not call the latter 'industrial therapy': we call it 'consultancy'. It is good to see that the term 'family consultancy' is being used by those who follow the work of the Milan Group (Palazzoli *et al.*, 1978), but it is also interesting to wonder why the term 'therapy' is not being used by industrial consultants.

The application of systems concepts to the family was a very important development. But I began to think that a more appropriate term for this new way of working would be 'systems problem-solving' rather than 'family therapy'. I think that it is; but the term 'problem-solving' has too much of a sense of control and certainty to feel right. Our work enables people to change and neither we nor they can predict how that will go; and that leads me to conclude that the term 'systems change' is a better description of the work which we attempt.

An alternative term is 'family systems' change' but this phrase implies that it is the family which has to change. Whilst 'family therapy' has very helpfully placed the individual in the context of the family, its exponents have not on the whole taken the next logical step of placing the family in *its* context. Just as the bizarre behaviour of an individual may be functional for the family, so also may the bizarre behaviour of a family be functional in the wider context. The inclusion of the word 'family' has the effect of avoiding a focus upon other systems. For example, Blaxter (1981) studied the relationship between health and what has been called 'cycles of deprivation'. She concluded '. . . it is clear that the major influences (on ill health in children) are still (air) pollution (and) economic disadvantage . . .' (p. 222). She also says, with regard to the relationship between childhood health and adult health,

> above all it is obvious that childhood accidents matter . . . it seems probable that the remedies lie in public policies regarding the environment – the control of traffic through housing estates, the elimination of fire-trap housing – rather than in the behaviour of individual families (p. 221).

The important point in this illustration is Blaxter's recognition that some remedies are not in the hands of individual families; only a collective approach to these problems will bring effective change.

This leads me to consider the environment of families; their 'supra-system', an idea which is, as yet, rarely present in the writings of family therapists. We talk about 'sub-system' and 'system' (with the system in practice being a family) – but not 'supra-system'. This must be a serious theoretical omission because it leads to a practice which inevitably lays responsibilities that belong elsewhere upon families. This theoretical omission also encourages a lack of interest by the helping professions in policies which affect the context – and which therefore, of course, affect the families which live in that context. The concept of 'equifinality' is related to this issue but is rarely used. 'According to this principle, a system can reach the same final state from differing initial positions and by a variety of paths' (Emery, 1969, p. 100). Two such paths may be by interventions at different system levels. For example, taking Blaxter's illustration, we may, by education and exhortation, enable parents at the level of one family to protect their child from a fire accident. If we intervene instead at the level of neighbourhood housing, we may not only protect children in that family but in other families as well.

Scheflen (1981) has developed a theoretical framework which, if followed in practice, can remove inappropriate burdens from the family. Scheflen considers schizophrenia at eight systems levels ranging from those of the neural systems of the body to that of the societal organisation. He posits an important principle, namely: 'A problem in dysfunction at any level of organisation is ideally corrected at higher levels of organisation' (p. 158). We have obviously taken seriously this principle in relation to individual dysfunction. What stops us taking it equally seriously at higher levels? I think that what in the main prevents us is that such systemic thinking and practice would challenge the linear thinking which generally pervades our society. In particular, I believe that it is the belief in the necessity of 'power' in ordering human society which would be most challenged by a systemic approach.

The issue of 'power'

There has been an important and unresolved disagreement between two major theorists, Gregory Bateson and Jay Haley with regard to the subject of 'power'. Bateson's view was that the concept is applicable to the physical world but not to the world of relationships. Referring to its use in relationships he wrote: 'Probably most people believe in it. It is a myth which, if everybody believes in it, becomes self-validating. But it is still epistemological lunacy and leads inevitably to various sorts of disasters' (Bateson, 1973, p. 462). What Bateson seems to mean is that as soon as we use words which fit the physical world rather than the world of creatures, we inevitably treat one another as objects. However, Haley has defended his use of the word 'power' on the grounds that human beings 'cannot not organise ... and that organisation is hierarchical' (Haley, 1976b, p. 78). They 'form a status, or power, ladder in which each creature has a place in the hierarchy' (Haley, 1976a, p. 101). I imagine that Bateson would have agreed with Haley's use of the word 'status' because it is a word which implies a difference in function, a difference which is reciprocal between different levels of the organisation. But it is Haley's acceptance of 'power' which Bateson regarded as dangerous. Bateson's view appears to be that 'power', 'force' and 'control' describe linear processes which at best can refer to bodies but not to persons; and that the danger of the myth of 'power' is that it can be regarded as an appropriate way of dealing with persons. I think that we are so imbued with this myth that it becomes difficult to imagine that a society in which 'power' is absent could be a safe one; that a society in which relationships are based upon service and the creative use of difference, is possible. Perhaps a balanced view of this debate is that we should, in general, adhere to Bateson's concern about the misuse of power, but to acknowledge that there are occasions in social life where its use by legitimate authorities becomes necessary. Thus the highest possible level of dialogue combined with the lowest possible level of the legitimated use of power might be the principle upon which government is exercised in a democracy.

The environment of families

Despite a considerable amount of supporting sociological evidence for the existence of a complex relationship between the family and other social institutions there are many family therapists who do not take this relationship sufficiently into account. I will refer briefly to three aspects of this relationship, namely the impact of occupation, of major societal changes and of social stratification.

Occupation

There is evidence which shows that, in quite direct ways, some occupations have a marked effect upon the structure and processes of the family. For example, Tunstall's (1962) study of fishermen analyses the impact of an occupation which involves men in being away from home for two weeks in every three and the problems arising from rapidly alternating role-allocation between husband and wife. One of Tunstall's findings was that the divorce rate amongst these men was twice that of other employed men in the same region. To regard marital problems as purely intra-familial in origin would be widely to miss the mark, for as Tunstall concludes 'the fisherman's marriage is shaped by his occupation' (p. 164). Another example of the impact of occupation is contained in a study of coal-miners. This study shows the way in which a dangerous occupation creates a situation where the relationships of the men involved are likely to contain high levels of interdependency and closeness. This closeness is at such a level that family relationships become secondary, even during the miners' leisure time. This is to a point where 'the whole life of the miner, under the influence of his group of friends, inhibits any display of tenderness and love in sexual relationships' (Dennis *et al.*, 1969). Both these studies show a direct relationship between occupation and family structure and processes.

Thus an issue here is whether work within a community (such as adult education and dialogue between families) is not more appropriate than working with single families.

Major societal change

Unfortunately sociological analysis at a macro-level does not easily lend itself to such clear-cut understandings of the relationship between the family and other social institutions. But that such a relationship exists is portrayed in the analyses of the impact of World War II upon the structure of the family, by Fletcher (1966) in Britain and by Lipman-Blumen (1975) in America. Lipman-Blumen shows that there was a decrease in the age of marriage, an increase in the number of women working, an entry by women into occupational roles previously held by men, and an increase in divorce rates. Fletcher confirms that a similar increase in divorce rates occurred in Britain and concluded that 'few people seem to realise how extensively the major wars of our time have disturbed human relationships at the most intimate level' (Fletcher, 1966).

A continuing aspect of British and American life which has emerged as one of major importance in recent years is the consistently high percentage of people who are unemployed. Some of the impact of unemployment upon family life was described in an early study entitled *Unemployment, Family Structure and Social Disorganisation* (National Advisory Commission on Civil Disorder, 1968). The authors concluded that:

If men stay at home without working, their inadequacies constantly confront them and tensions arise between them and their wives and children. Under these pressures, it is not surprising that many of these men flee their responsibilities as husbands and fathers.

Recent British books (Hayes and Nutman, 1981; and Fagin and Little, 1984) have outlined the extent to which unemployment correlates with ill-health, lowered self-esteem and change in family roles. Their findings show that the intra-familial focus of much family therapy is much too limited a focus in such situations, and may be almost irrelevant to many of them.

Social stratification

One of the central aspects of low social class is that it correlates with a number of material factors which are thought to be relevant to physical, emotional and intellectual development. This is shown in the extensive research programme of the National Child Development Study into 16,000 children born in 1958. Davie *et al.* (1972, p. 57) state that 'The results have demonstrated clearly the relationship between poor housing amenities and overcrowding on the one hand and on the other hand educational performance and social adjustment in school . . .' Utilising the same sample, Wedge and Prosser (1973) applied three criteria which, when present together were described as representing 'social disadvantage'. These were low income, poor housing and atypical family composition (such as single-parent household or a large number of children). There were significant differences between this category and the remainder of the sample. Whilst one in every nine of the socially disadvantaged children were received into the care of public agencies, this happened to only one in a hundred amongst the rest of the sample; and the experience of chronic illness or disability amongst socially disadvantaged fathers was four times that of non-disadvantaged fathers.

Ferri's (1976) research into the one-parent families in the NCDS sample notes that the school attainment and social adjustment of the children in these families compared unfavourably with the rest of the sample and concluded that '... their relatively poor showing owed much more to the disadvantaging circumstances associated with one-parent status (such as poor housing and financial hardship) than to the fact of being brought up by a lone mother or father.'

This kind of evidence indicates that with many families who are designated as being lower social class it is essential that the helping professions place an increasing emphasis upon invervention into environmental conditions.

Of relevance here is the fact that a very high proportion of the population served by the helping professions, at least in Britain, are of low social class. For example, the research by Nursten and colleagues (1972) into the clients of all social workers in Bradford found that the social class (where known) of the chief economic supporter of client families was disproportionately either lower class or unemployed. This was especially so with regard to problems involving children. Childcare officers and education welfare officers had only 1 per cent of clients in classes I and II (Registrar-General's classification) whilst family service unit workers and moral welfare workers had none. This latter situation was also true of the probation service. Social workers in other settings, namely mental health, child guidance and medical social work had about 6 per cent of their clients in these two classes.

Wedge and Prosser (1973) also note the very high rate of involvement of their 'socially disadvantaged' group with social workers. Although they consisted of only 1:16 of the population, they accounted for 2:5 of those who were involved with children's departments and the probation service.

Dilemmas of the therapist

Knowledge about social influences on behaviour places family therapists in two principal dilemmas. The first is that, whilst such knowledge might indicate the necessity to change other systems, therapists have limited ability to effect such change. Second, although collaboration with other systems may be necessary to bring about changes in the family, the cost of such collaboration may be the therapist's involvement in a process of control.

Since the helping professions have become 'big business', questions have, rightly, been asked about their effectiveness in alleviating human problems. Whilst some researches indicate effectiveness, a substantial number do not. In 1971 a conference was held at Fordham University to assess the reasons for these differences. The conclusions were complex but can be summarised as follows: that effective interventions occurred when clients and helpers were agreed upon the task to be tackled and set time-limits on their work together; that ineffective interventions occurred when the helpers attempted to work within face-to-face systems, even though it was apparent that the cause of the problem lay *outside* these systems. Contributors to the symposium regarded poverty, racial and social class discrimination, sub-standard housing, unemployment, poor education facilities and different kinds of social stigmatisation as being amongst such causes, and attested to 'the futility of attempting to resolve our major social problems through micro-system intervention' (Mullen and Dumpson, 1972). This view may have considerable significance in explaining the high drop-out rate from family therapy of families of low socio-economic circumstances (Slipp *et al.*, 1974).

It is to the credit of family therapists that much of their approach is within the time-limited and target-focussed framwork. In addition, a small but important minority have not only ventured into wider systems but have developed exciting methods of intervention. Amongst these are the network therapists, (Speck and Attneave, 1973; Speck and Rueveni, 1969), and those like Auerswald (1971), Garrison (1974), Erickson *et al.* (1974) and Dimmock and Dungworth (1983, 1985), who work with the family and representatives of other systems. Work on the interface between family and school systems has been described by Aponte (1976), Skynner (1976) and Dowling (1985), and Palazzoli (1983 and 1985) has written about the application of a systemic perspective to work in the community with people who are designated as 'mentally ill'. She has also produced interesting work describing the snares which can face us when working within, and between, work organisations (Palazzoli, 1984). Dimmock and Dungworth (1983, 1985) have shown how the staff of British Social Services Departments can unwittingly create and maintain difficulties in the lives of their clients, and have demonstrated how statutory responsibilities can be incorporated within a systemic framework (Dimmock and Dungworth, 1983). They have more recently described an important development of this statutory work, namely bringing the network of helping professionals and the family together. They have shown how this approach can not only clarify goals and reduce confusion, but can be extraordinarily fruitful in its outcome (Dimmock and Dungworth, 1985).

However, what is largely unexplored in the writing of those who work across the boundary between the family and the outside world is the authority by which they intervene. Those who have developed network therapy in the United States appear to cope with their lack of authority by having the nuclear family both convene the network and collect the fee. Others manage by inviting representatives of other systems to attend, with no reference being made to the sanctions which might be applied if these representatives decline the invitation. The missing housing manager or DHSS representative may in some situations be more significant than the missing family member.

Perhaps the most striking feature of accounts of work across the family boundary is the absence of a political perspective; or sometimes, the presence of a desperate attempt to be apolitical. Auerswald (1971) noted the despair of many who grasp the inter-relatedness of social problems 'because without the support of those in positions of power, they cannot get on with the task' (p. 265). The logic of this is that politicians become an important target for therapists and families, but for some reason Auerswald took a different view, namely that therapists should become 'post-political' and so avoid 'the trap of politicisation' (p. 266). What he appears to mean by this is that they should take a view which recognises the inter-relatedness of everything. However, he then seems to move to a different dimension by assuming that this recognition leads to an overcoming of sectional interests and factions. Auerswald is deeply aware of an ecological perspective on human problems; his apolitical stance is therefore puzzling because it seems that politics is, *par excellence*, the occupation which has to take an ecological perspective. Intervention in any system, including the family, is always a political intervention in as much as it is aimed at changing or maintaining the distribution of resources. In this sense to attempt to be post-political is in fact to be pre-political.

David Donnison, in the inaugural lecture instituted by *Community Care* (1984) put matters clearly and succinctly when he said that we should start

> From a concern about suffering, exploitation, unfairness, the blighting of human potentialities and the corruption of human relationships – in a word 'poverty'. If we meet critics we should ask them if they deny the *existence* of these evils, or deny that they can be *remedied*, or deny that they *are evils*. If they deny none of these things we can start talking – arguing perhaps – about remedies. There will always be at least one alternative to any course of action we may propose: the alternative of doing nothing. Present arrangements – the status quo – have powerful defenders. They would not have lasted so long if they did not suit a lot of people pretty well (p. 18).

Donnison is referring to poverty in Britain. If we cannot alter that, how can we even *contemplate* the changes which are necessary to bring about a redistribution of resources in favour of the Third World? And this question makes us confront the even more difficult one that, in a context of widespread destitution, starvation and ill-health, which is the lot of the majority in the developing world, family therapy has no meaning or relevance at all.

Employing organisations

It is necessary first to refer to important differences between the United States and Britain with regard to the organisational aspects of the helping professions. In Britain most people who practise family therapy are employed within state organisations, whilst in America many more are self-employed or employed by private organisations, which may or may not be in receipt of funds from the state. Whilst most of the references in this section are British, the ideas they contain have a clear, if more indirect, relevance to the American setting also.

It is important to consider the extent to which employing organisations are expressions of social control. One of the facts of life for people in the British helping professions is that almost all their members are employed by state organisations such as the National Health Service, local authority Social Services Departments and the Probation and After-Care Service. These organisations are directly influenced by politicians, who in turn respond to the formal authority of the majority or to the informal influence of elites and pressure groups. It would, in this situation, be surprising if the employees of these organisations were not expected to uphold the norms of these categories. The laws under which psychiatrists and social workers function contain clear powers for controlling people (HMSO, 1948 and 1983) and whilst these may apply directly to only a part of their work, they inevitably influence all relationships between these professions and their clients. Even where their work is not underpinned by the law, these professions are still involved in attempting to change social situations. One would imagine that the direction of such change would be a matter of vital interest, yet Barbara Wootton's comments referring to social work and written in 1959 could almost stand unaltered today:

> If the purpose of social casework is to encourage in others attributes and behaviour conformable to particular norms, then the obligation to examine those norms and to make them explicit becomes imperative. Of this, however, in the literature of social work there is as yet little sign (p. 283).

The inclusion of control as an aspect of the activity of members of these professions does not mean the exclusion of caring. Rather it acknowledges that the role of the helper who is based in a state organisation is a highly ambiguous one. Neither does the inclusion of control signify something which is necessarily unacceptable or unjust. All societies have systems of control and what is important is that they are open to rational examination, especially to the question: 'Is the control system aimed at everybody, or a part of society only? It may be that this question is more in the open in Britain than it is in the United States, where the relationship between the helping professions and social control is more blurred. To take another example from social work, a very influential American social work text by Pincus and Minahan (1973) contains no references to social control when listing the purposes of social work but later includes it as an effect of social work practice. It does not appear to relate to their list of purposes and seems to be brought in almost as an unfortunate side-effect. In the literature of family therapy whilst the term is conspicuous by its absence, the reality to which the term refers is often uncomfortably present.

Whatever the organisational setting of the family therapist she faces one common problem, namely the lack of a legal right to intervene in systems. This contrasts sharply with the presence of authority to intervene with individuals. The helping professions have in general worked within a model which regards the causes of a person's symptoms as within the person. To change this tradition is difficult enough but it becomes almost insuperable when one takes into account the fact that the traditional individualistic view of aetiology is in fact underwritten by statute. It is individuals, not families or other systems, who are committed to mental hospital or placed on probation. And however much the helping professions begin to take the view that an individual's behaviour is functional for a system, they have almost no legal basis upon which to follow this through. Thus, when these professions become involved in family or other social systems they do so on the authority of their knowledge, skill and personal values, not by that of the law.

Ethical issues

Many of the ethical dilemmas which emerge are implicit in what has been said so far, but in conclusion I would like to make them explicit:

1   Do families 'take the blame' for behaviours and illnesses which clearly have wider social and structural causes?
2   Do therapists seek to reduce the oppression which is signified by poverty, or collude with it?
3   Do therapists challenge the cultural definitions of stigma which are applied to many of the families with which they work – or do they take part in applying those definitions?
4   Do therapists uphold the general professional ethic of putting clients' interests first or do they enter into collaborative alliances with other

agencies to the detriment of the family's autonomy?
5   By concentrating her intervention on the family system, when causative factors exist in other systems, does the family therapist do more harm to the family than good?

10

ETHICS, PROFESSIONALISM AND FAMILY THERAPISTS

Douglas Haldane

Introduction

My intention in this chapter is to examine ways in which some professions express their concern about ethical issues in practice and to explore some of these issues, together with problems involved in developing codes of practice.

My perspective is that of a psychiatrist, with no formal schooling in ethics, but constantly faced with ethical problems in practice. As an undergraduate and in postgraduate training, I was influenced by seniors whose clinical practice was informed and constrained by concern for the dignity of their patients; by their awareness of patients' rights and freedoms and by their sense of responsibility to their patients. These attitudes were focussed then, as they still are in medical work generally, on individuals. The conceptual framework which informed my early training drew attention to the interaction of biological, psychological and social factors in the causes and management of psychiatric disorders (Meyer, 1957). Later experience, particularly work with families in a department of child and family psychiatry, was influenced by psychodynamic theory and what had come to be called systems theory (Haldane *et al.*, 1980). While recognising that there can be debate about the understanding and meaning of terms, what has remained constant is the view that fundamental to our ethical concerns should be the autonomy, freedoms, rights and responsibilities of the individual, in the context of his or her relationships, whatever their structural or institutional form.

In seeking a starting point from which to explore ethics and professional practice I adapt and quote from Dunstan (1981). What he says of ethics in relation to medical practice is of general application, ethics being those obligations of a moral nature which govern practice, the common possession of a profession's practitioners who, alike by colleagues and by society, are expected to adhere to them in their personal exercise of these obligations. Professional ethics subordinate knowledge and technical skill to helping and govern the relationship between practitioner and client(s). Their purpose is to create and maintain trust: of clients in their practitioner; of practitioners in each other and of society in the profession corporately. Help offered is 'conditioned by a fundamental belief that the respect due to human beings is not diminished by their dependency, their "client" status, their human need'. Further, with respect to continuity,

> it is the responsibility of the profession to develop its ethics to accommodate new demands and circumstances not encountered before; to transmit its ethics to each new generation of practitioners; to help and sustain its members in the practice of their profession; and to discipline them when, by unethical conduct, they deny to their clients the standard of service they may properly expect, or violate trust, and so damage public confidence in the profession as a whole (Dunstan, 1981).

Present position: the professions compared

Doctors (particularly psychiatrists) social workers, psychologists, nurses, personnel trained in psychotherapy and counselling, contribute to the practice of family therapy. In describing public positions on the ethical aspects of practice, I shall focus on the first three of these professions, in order to illustrate some similarities and differences; and on the Association for Family Therapy, which has a multi-disciplinary membership.

The medical profession

Of these professions, the medical profession has the longest history of debate about ethical issues and has in recent years become more the object of public scrutiny than the others. The General Medical Council (GMC) was established under the Medical Act 1858. Since then its constitution, duties and powers have evolved and developed, leading in 1983 to the most recent Medical Act. Registration with the GMC is a necessary pre-requisite to the right to practise. The Council now has responsibilities to oversee both undergraduate and postgraduate training of doctors, thus having power to ensure their competence to practise. It has disciplinary functions and from time to time it issues guidelines about the ethical aspects of medical practice.

Before the British Medical Association (BMA) was founded in 1856 the Association which was its fore-runner had, in 1849, appointed a committee on medical ethics. The most recent addition of the BMA's *Handbook of Medical Ethics* (1984) has sections on the relationships between doctors and individuals; the relationships between doctors, groups in society, the state and the media; on etiquette, professional discipline and the law; on ethical dilemmas and on ethical codes and statements. While it has its limitations, because no such document can be fully comprehensive, it does offer guidelines on a wide range of issues arising in practice. The Association's journal, *The British Medical Journal*, has in recent years carried many articles on ethical matters and has actively promoted the necessary debate; but while all doctors must be registered with the GMC, not all are members of the BMA.

The Journal of Medical Ethics, published quarterly, was established in 1974 'to promote the study of contemporary medico-moral problems and to influence the quality of both professional and public discussion' (Shotter, 1981). A *Dictionary of Medical Ethics* was first published in 1977 with a revised and enlarged edition in 1981 (Duncan *et al.*, 1981). Edited by professors of medical education, of moral and social theology and of surgical endocrinology, its 149 contributors offer a wide range of information and material for debate. Also published in 1981 was *Psychiatric Ethics* (Bloch and Chodoff, 1981) edited by psychiatrists from Oxford and Washington (USA) and with contributions from a further 16 authors.

None of these publications, and this is not offered as a complete list, refers to ethical issues in relation to what in medical parlance would be called clinical work with families. This is a surprising and regrettable omission, because it fails to take account of family-related aspects of clinical practice as well as of developments in the field of family therapy.

Social workers

It is not clear whether social work is to be regarded as a profession because some social workers are antagonistic to their being described as professional. Certainly there is no professional council which is the equivalent of the General Medical Council. I understand that the British Association of Social Workers (BASW) is even less representative of social workers than the British Medical Association is of practising doctors. BASW publishes a *Code of Ethics for Social Work*, adopted at its AGM in 1975, all members being 'required to uphold the code'. Its primary objective 'is to make these implicit principles (i.e. of ethics) explicit for the protection of clients'. The foreword is concerned mainly with the obligations of social workers in their professional practice. It goes on to a Statement of Principles, a section on the Principles of Practice and then comments on these three statements. Significantly it states that the 'social worker's basic values must relate to individuals, whether he works with individuals, groups or committees, since it is the welfare of the individuals in a group or community which is the social worker's basic concern, even if indirectly'. With its focus on individuals, this code is at one with those for doctors and for psychologists. More recently BASW has published a set of discussions of issues which arise in putting the code into practice (Watson, 1985).

Psychologists

Psychologists, however they are described, clinical, educational, academic, etc., are not required to register with a council, nor are they required to be members of the British Psychological Society (BPS). Among documents relevant to this chapter's discussion, the BPS has published *Ethical Principles for Research with Human Subjects* (1978); *Guidelines for the Professional Practice of Clinical Psychology* (1983) and *A Code of Conduct for Psychologists* (1985).

The Association for Family Therapy

Like the other organisations mentioned, this multi-disciplinary association of practitioners of family therapy in Britain is not fully representative of those engaged in such work. Founded in 1976, it did not form a sub-committee on ethics till 1981.

Its 'house journal', the *Newsletter*, first issued in 1976, has contained a number of articles on ethical and related matters. Responding to the then working party on the registration of psychotherapists, the chairman considered it appropriate that family therapy in general, though not the practice of therapists, become eventually subject to a code of ethics (*Newsletter*, 1979). The convener of the sub-committee on training (*Newsletter*, 1980) raised issues and offered guidelines about ethical problems (not least those of confidentiality) in relation to video recording of family sessions, live supervision, the use of the one-way screen and training groups – guidelines which have been adopted by many practitioners.

On behalf of the Association, the *Journal of Family Therapy* was first published in 1979. In its first 28 isues there have been only two articles with an explicitly philosophical title (Haldane and McCluskey, 1982; and Tuson, 1985) and none explicitly on ethical issues. Consideration of these is singularly lacking in the context of articles, though one on 'The struggle for control in family therapy: a means to an end or an end in itself?' has a section headed 'Ethical Considerations' (Dowling, 1985).

The Association's Sub-Committee on Ethics organised and reported in the *Newsletter* (1983) two workshops whose members were practitioners of family therapy, philosophers and theologians. It made available to the membership a list of philosophers and others schooled in ethics who were willing to explore with practitioners their ethical concerns. To what extent such opportunities have been used has not been monitored. In its earlier discussions the Sub-Committee, responding to what it perceived to be the general view of the membership, thought it inappropriate to prepare and publish a code of ethics. But there has been a change. In its report to the Association's 1985 AGM, the Sub-Committee intimated that such an exercise had begun, in response to enquiries and pressures from members and others, to develop a statement of ethics and guidelines. As a first step, the Sub-Committee will be considering conduct, competency, consent and confidentiality (*Newsletter*, 1985). This may lead eventually to an acceptance that practitioners must be able to justify their actions, not only in terms of knowledge and skills but also ethically; and that the influence of their ethical standards should be as subject to scrutiny and evaluation as the methods and techniques which they use.

Ethical issues in practice

Competence to practise, approval, registration

If an activity, or those who practise it, is to be described as professional, there must be some way of assessing or examining competence to practise. This requires descriptions and definitions about the knowledge and skills required to become basically competent, about the forms, methods and content of the training required to achieve this level of competence, together with structures and procedures which allow professionals and public alike to be aware of the setting, maintenance and evaluation of standards. Such structures and procedures exist in the councils which govern these matters in relation to the education and training of doctors, nurses and social workers and for clinical psychologists in the British Psychological Society. But none of these governing bodies so far requires competence in the practice of family therapy in those who have completed basic training.

My experience is that, among practitioners of family therapy in the United Kingdom, attention to these matters is characterised more by competition and rivalry than by agreement on basic principles. While the Association for Family Therapy has not yet reached formal agreement about the basic skills required for practice, it has for some years tried to define policies and procedures for the approval of training courses, the number of which has steadily increased. The best efforts of its Sub-Committee on Approval have so far been in vain, as its convener pessimistically concludes in his report to the Association's 1985 AGM (*Newsletter*, 1985).

Even when agreement is reached on the definition of standards of competence and training and on their evaluation, professionals may need in addition to consider the question of registration. Doctors, nurses and practitioners in the 'professions supplementary to medicine' are required to be registered with their councils, which have statutory powers, rights and obligations. Such registration confers on practitioners the right to independent practice, the obligation to maintain accepted standards and the possibility of having these rights and privileges modified or withdrawn.

Among the practitioners of psychotherapy and counselling the issue of registration has been actively debated since the publication of the Foster Report (1971). This report was followed by that of a Professions Joint Working Party (Sieghart, 1978) which made a variety of recommendations. In turn, this led to meetings between the Department of Health and Social Security and organisations with an interest in the statutory registration of psychotherapists. Yet another consequence was a now yearly series of conferences, organised by the British Association of Counselling, attended by representatives of the many and varied interested groups, leading to productive debate on training and the ethics of practice, but not to agreement on the issue of registration. Whether the deliberations of the psychotherapy and counselling organisations are of relevance for, or acceptable to, practitioners of family therapy is debatable. Among such practitioners many do not consider that the term 'therapy' is an appropriate description of what they do. Those who seek to find another descriptive title would not countenance the idea that they should be included in organisations which accept titles such as 'therapy' or 'counselling'.

Moral and practice autonomy

The greater part of this section draws heavily upon the entry on Moral Autonomy (Campbell, 1981) in the *Dictionary of Medical Ethics*, Duncan *et al.* (1981). 'Autonomy' refers to the capacity for, or right to, self-determination and 'moral autonomy' to willing what is right, out of respect for universal law. Such autonomy is to be distinguished from 'heteronomy' (acting under external influence or duress); from 'libertarianism' (acting in any way one chooses) and from 'individualism' (assertion of one's right against those of others). 'The phrase "respect for persons" is often used to express the notion of safe-guarding *every* individual's integrity (including one's own) which is the central feature of this ethical approach' (Campbell, 1981; see also Lindley, chapter 7 in this volume).

> Criticisms of the concept come from Determinism (the view that every human action is causally determined) and Social Benefit Theory (the view that good consists in maximising the benefit of the majority). According to the former, freedom is an illusion and the concept of autonomy vacuous. According to the latter, personal liberty may impede the good of society as a whole and therefore cannot be regarded as a moral absolute. A combination of these views would put forward the ideal of efficient social conditioning to maximise happiness as an alternative to individual autonomy (Campbell, 1981).

These issues are relevant to family therapy. A focus on families rather than on individuals could be construed as a form of 'social conditioning', just as attempts to politicise work with families might be regarded as a form of 'social engineering' (see Kingston's discussion in chapter 9 of this volume).

'Autonomy in the doctor-patient relationship is safeguarded by professional independence on the one hand and consent to treatment on the other' (Campbell, 1981). Given that a major trend in the development of family therapy is that a team of colleagues works with a family, e.g. when one member is in actual contact with the family and other members of the team are behind a one-way screen or observing on a television monitor, we must ask who carries the necessary professional independence? And in the case of the family, who has the right and responsibility to give consent to 'treatment'? These matters are further elaborated in later sections, together with issues of confidentiality, record-keeping and research.

Doctors in general claim the right to retain what is called clinical autonomy, the right, without undue interference from others, to take decisions about the assessment or treatment of their patients, on the grounds that they have and are charged with the ultimate responsibility for making the relevant decisions. But this principle within medical practice is being challenged. Patients increasingly wish to share in decision-making and may claim the right to have the final say. Colleagues, including other professionals, may claim the right to consensus decision-making. Pressure groups express the need and wish to be consulted about, and involved in, many aspects of medical care. Families too should have the final say about whether they can accept or refuse help offered, even when such help is offered by a team, not by an individual. What will happen when pressure groups, which may be seen as networks of clients, demand the right for families to involve networks of professionals in responding to their needs?

Issues such as the autonomy of individuals in families, particularly that of non-adult members; of the practice autonomy of teams; of the professional autonomy of individual members of teams have been insufficiently addressed (but see McCluskey's discussion in chapter 4 of this volume).

Trust and power

The life experience of some families may be such that they cannot put their trust in others and more specifically, they may have found some professionals to be untrustworthy; while others will retain trust as an expectation or hope. For the professional, it is one thing to be trusted, another to feel deserving of that trust, especially if the organisational setting of the work limits the professional's autonomy.

An important aspect of this trust is not to abuse the potential power which accompanies it. Families can be said to have the right to reject what the therapist has to offer, but this of itself does not minimise the therapist's potential power: the therapist determines many of the conditions in which encounters with families take place and some techniques of family therapy do not include discussing with families their aims. There is always the danger that the exercise of power, whether or not recognised or admitted, will over-ride the legitimate interests of a family or of its individual members. This risk can be lessened only if recognised and adequately monitored (see McCluskey, chapter 4 of this volume).

Responsibility and accountability

Issues of responsibility and accountability can be defined in terms of management or of organisational systems and dynamics. They are also terms which carry ethical connotations.

While families do have a degree of responsibility for deciding on what changes they seek and for the process of change which develops in their encounter with a professional worker, the latter carries a responsibility greater and beyond that of the families worked with. Implicitly or explicitly, family therapists claim confidence in promoting change in the interests of families; confidence in their own approach and method and a capacity to foresee the likely consequences of the work. They are responsible for their actions, not only in general, but in each encounter – consequences which affect families, therapists, the professionals or organisations of which they are a part. No debate, discussion or exploration of the dynamics of family-therapist interaction can deny this responsibility of the therapist.

Family therapists are also accountable for the exercise of this responsibility. First, they are accountable to the families with whom they work, in general to give primacy to the rights and needs of the families, to use their best endeavours in the interests of the families. Such accountability carries the risk of the therapist being criticised by peers, or employing organisation, or the law, or society at large. Secondly, the therapist is accountable as employee, professional and citizen. Such accountability is not only about 'reporting upwards' in an organisational hierarchy: it is also about the possibility of being called to account for actions, about taking the consequences.

To be responsible for one's actions and accountable in so many ways can lead to anxiety, uncertainty and conflict. Employers and professional councils may define basic standards of practice and competence. Employers cannot define ethical standards; and while professional councils may provide guidelines to the ethical aspects of practice, how these are understood and interpreted are conclusions to which the individual professional can be held responsible.

Consent in relation to intervention, training and research

Doctors are increasingly exhorted to ensure that persons in the role of patients are sufficiently informed about diagnosis and about the nature and consequences of treatment prescribed, particularly in relation to possible risks and side effects. Such responsibility has become particularly important in psychiatric practice, especially in relation to consent to treatment by patients detained in hospital and on the basis of some legal procedure. Such responsibility requires of practitioners that they be fully and sufficiently aware of the nature, purpose and consequences of actions taken by them or on their advice. It has to be said also that patients, or the parents of young children, also have responsibilities in accepting or rejecting the advice or prescription.

How are we to view the issue of consent within the framework of the practice of family therapy? If we are to accept the kind of responsibilities described above this would involve, at least, practitioners explaining the nature, methods and aims of their particular approach and the accompanying risks. Such a practice requires an openness which is not evident in all current techniques of family therapy. How and from whom might one obtain valid consent? If the autonomy and rights of individual members of the family are to be respected, what kind of consent is acceptable: a corporate consent of all members or, especially where there are young children, only from the parents? In a family, who has the responsibility for giving consent? In turn, who can accept valid consent? Registered medical practitioners carry that responsibility as individuals. What of the situation where the practitioner negotiating with the family is one of a team, the others being not visible because they are observers, or when a senior colleague is in another office? And what about consent in relation to research? Admittedly, in the United Kingdom research in family therapy is still limited, but family therapists as such do not presently have available the kind of guidelines and clear procedures seen as essential for research in medicine or clinical psychology. This is an issue which has not yet been formally addressed by the Research Sub-Committee of the Association for Family Therapy.

Confidentiality, record-keeping and privilege

A consequence of the trust which most families bring to a first encounter is their assumption that what happens will remain confidential and that information will be shared with others only with their permission and only if considered to be in their best interests. Information will be contained in records which can and may be used not only directly in relation to work with the family, but also for other purposes. These include standards of care, practice management, research, legal actions. The debate about the rights of patients, clients and families to have open access to their records is accompanied by debate about which other personnel should have access and for what purpose. In these general aspects, records about families are no different from those about individuals. But in the case of families, who has the right to give consent to release of information; what happens if one member refuses consent and what is the position when someone not working with the family uses records to collect information about one individual and can then find information about other(s) which might be inappropriately used? I presume that with regard to disclosure of information in actions before the Courts, those who work with families are in the same position as medical practitioners, i.e. they have no privilege and if so directed, must divulge confidential information or else risk being charged with contempt of court. The desire for increased openness and accessibility of record systems may place a great strain on the system of confidentiality and on the application to practice of ethical principles.

Team work and ethical responsibilities

One major development in family therapy is that therapists work in teams, many of them interdisciplinary, a way of working which poses problems of accountability and responsibility, not least in relation to ethical issues.

I can best indicate how such problems may develop by reference to relatively recent history in medical practice. The medical profession has a long history of working closely with members of other professions, most of whom, in the National Health Service (NHS) reorganisation of the 1970s were described as 'professions supplementary to medicine'. Both the GMC and the BMA, while recognising the value to patient care of interdisciplinary collaboration, enjoin doctors to undertake the role of team leader and not to delegate responsibility without ensuring that they retain ultimate control and supervision. This wish to retain power and control is being increasingly challenged in professional, administrative and political terms. The reorganisations of the Health Service and of local authority services in the 1970s led to members of the different professions within multidisciplinary teams being accountable to different management structures and hierarchies, who claimed different rights about the nature and degree of control which should be exercised over professional staff in contact with patients. These changes were not accompanied by any clarification about which profession or person should hold ultimate responsibility or carry the final accountability (and to whom) for the professional work of the team. In my view, these administrative, organisational and managerial changes both expressed and fuelled the inter-professional competition, rivalry and envy about who had the right, or freedom, or power, to do what and also heightened conflicts about who is most competent to perform which tasks. They led to a fragmentation of care, a process not likely to be reversed by more recent changes of management policy and practice within the NHS. I do not see any evidence that multidisciplinary teams of family therapists, whatever their organisational base, have overcome these problems. Nor have the ethical issues been sufficiently addressed, for reasons which are developed in the section which follows.

Ethical codes, discipline and professionalisation

Whether or not ethical codes can or should be introduced to govern or guide the practice of family therapists and how these would influence the work and collaboration of colleagues from different professions working within family therapy teams, is inextricably linked with the question of whether there should be organised a profession of family therapy. Subscription to a code of ethics and acceptance of related discipline, would be of limited value unless the defining organisation also had other powers and responsibilities, e.g. to prescribe and monitor criteria and programmes for basic training (perhaps leading to some form of registration) and for continuing or post-basic training; and to define acceptable standards of practice. At present in the United Kingdom, the only organisation which could promote the necessary discussion and recommendations is the Association for Family Therapy. But not all who work as family therapists are members of the Association; not all practitioners would agree that the term 'family therapy' is appropriate to what they do and so far the Association has not considered it part of its task to seek to govern practice.

There is among practitioners of family therapy a deep division of opinion on these matters. There are a number of reasons for this division. The theories and practises of family therapy are not the development of any one profession: they do not, as it were, 'belong' to medicine or social work or psychology or any other professional group. They developed partly as an extension of other kinds of therapeutic work; partly as an expression of dissatisfaction with the existing theories and practice; even as a rebellion against the focus on individuals and on their intrapsychic experiences or behaviours. The shift to a focus on the family as a system led inevitably to an appreciation of the family as part of a network of systems; of the family influenced by its social context; and in turn to a political view of the 'causes' of family dysfunction and of the best means of alleviating this. Thus among practitioners are those who wish to concentrate on so-called 'therapeutic' work with families and others whose insights lead them to recommend a wider, more socio-political perspective for action (see Kingston, chapter 9 in this volume).

Within the Association for Family Therapy, the debate on the profession-alisation of family therapy was for some years relatively muted, but from 1984 became more overt, explicit, even clamorous, in meetings and in contributions to the Association's *Newsletter* (*Newsletter*, 1985). Any attempt at summary risks oversimplification of complex and emotionally charged arguments, but it seems that there are four points of view: (1) family therapists should be organised into a profession; (2) professionalisation should be resisted and an open, flexible system maintained; (3) family therapists should not be organised into a profession, because practitioners should undertake such work within the context of their existing professional discipline, e.g. social work, medicine (particularly psychiatry), psychology; (4) a new profession, not to be called family therapy, should be organised. These four points of view will be briefly described.

Some advocate the development of a profession of family therapy for the practice of which would be required a nationally agreed training with oversight by an elected or appointed central organisation. Such a development, it is argued, would enhance standards of work; would allow members of other professions and the public at large to identify qualified practitioners; would provide practitioners with an appropriate career structure and would endow them with a recognisable status from which further responsibilities and powers would develop. If there were to be such changes, they would require also that potential employing organisations formally recognise such a profession, accept its standards and criteria and agree on appropriate conditions of salary and service.

There is, however, a strong body of opinion opposed to such recommendations. (Pilalis, 1984; *Newsletter*, 1985). Objectors assume that organisation of a profession of family therapy would become overconcerned with status and power; with self-regulation and self-seeking; with the wish to retain knowledge and expertise within its own boundaries, while denying this to others and with exclusiveness. Those who share this view seek to become facilitators of change, sharing their expertise and skill with others, rather than become experts who wish to confine knowledge and experience to a particular group of personnel, however registered or accredited.

Yet another group (*Newsletter*, 1980, 1985) argue that as family therapy, despite its various conceptual frameworks, methods and techniques, constitutes a particular kind of approach to individuals in their relationships within institutionalised systems, it can and should be practised within the boundaries of existing professions and of the agencies and services in which they are currently employed.

There is yet another point of view: that the argument for or against a profession of family therapy is irrelevant and that we must consider the needs of families in a much wider context. Such ideas have been discussed in an Editorial of the *Journal of Family Therapy* (1981) introducing papers by Jordan, Rochford, Reiger and Kraemer and by Kingston (1982 and *Newsletter*, 1985), ideas which lead to the possibility of the development of a new profession which would include those currently called therapists, conciliators, mediators, organisational consultants, conflict resolution personnel and those with similar roles in international disputes. Kingston (*Newsletter*, 1985) notes:

What these diverse occupations have in common are areas of theory, methods of practice and values, e.g. they all utilise systems concepts, theories about communication and information control, and have a distinct interest in process as well as content; they all use methods of joining with disputants, negotiating between them, and maintaining neutrality in their attempts to enable others to resolve their conflicts; and their values are likely to espouse the setting of goals by the disputants (unless a legal obligation makes that impossible), an equity in points of view being heard, a respect for differences, an openness about aspirations, a caring for persons, and a belief that everyone in a dispute can win, in the sense of living more creatively, and humanly.

Given such a range of options and aspirations, it is highly unlikely that the inherent conflicts can be resolved within the foreseeable future or that all practitioners of family therapy will be satisfied with the result. My hopes and expectations are limited, believing that we can move only gradually, rather than in a revolutionary way, towards new professional institutions. I hope that the Association for Family Therapy will take upon itself the authority to define standards of training and practice; to approve and evaluate programmes of training; to define an ethical code of practice and sanctions against transgression of such a code and that these definitions will inform practice whether family therapy practitioners remain within existing professional boundaries or seek to expand these in the search for a new and wider endeavour.

NOTES

1 Family therapy, attachment theory and general systems theory: separation may be no loss

1 In my judgment the price cannot be paid, but this may be premature. The grounds for Strawson's descriptions of human social life are rather special. See Strawson, 1959, pp. 9–12; Downie, 1966; Graham, 1977.

2. These extended territorial claims of systemic explanation are usually asserted not argued. Advocates more often detail successful clinical reliance on such a framework. Thus the assertion is supported. But such support as this reported experience gives is of limited value, given that their descriptions of changes experienced presuppose the appropriateness of the form of explanation espoused.

8 The language of objectivity and the ethics of reframing

1 Because our experiments aim to test laws which will operate 'other things being equal'; since other things rarely oblige us by being equal naturally, we set up experimental conditions to make sure they are; but social realities are always too complexly interwoven with 'other things' for such an operation to be possible.

2 I have in mind the cases of the man who could not get an erection and the insomniac, referred to by Brian Cade (1979). In these cases the injunction not to try is clearly meant to remove the anxiety which is the real obstacle.

3 Here I have in mind the three cases of 'helpless' women described by Brian

Cade (1979). I am in general agreement with Richard Lindley's fuller discussion of those case reports, as set out in chapter 7 in the present volume.

4 'Second-order discourse', i.e. talking about talking, rather than talking about the world.

5 On systems in a family context see Collier, 1977; and more generally about the nature of systems, see the passages on dialectic in Collier, 1979.

BIBLIOGRAPHY

Adler, A. (1928), *Understanding Human Nature*, Humanities Press, Atlantic Highlands, N.J., 1962.

Anderson, C. and Stewart, S. (1983), *Mastering Resistance: a practical guide to family therapy*, New York, Guildford Press.

Anscombe, G.E.M. (1975), 'Causation and Determination', in Sosa, E. (ed), *Causation and Conditionals*, Oxford, Oxford University Press.

Aponte, H. (1976), 'The family – school interview: an ecostructural approach', *Family Process*, 15.

Armstrong, D. (1982), 'The doctor-patient relationship: 1930–1980', in P. Wright and A. Treacher (eds), *The Problem of Medical Knowledge*, London, Routledge & Kegan Paul.

Auerswald, E. (1971), 'Families, change and the ecological perspective', *Family Process*, 10.

Bachrach, L.L. (1975), 'Marital status and mental disorder: an analytical review', *U.S. Department of Mental Health, Education and Welfare Report*, Maryland, Baltimore.

Bandler, R. and Grinder, J. (1976), *Structure of Magic*, vols 1 and 2, Palo Alto, Science and Behaviour Books.

Bateson, G. (1973), *Steps to an Ecology of Mind*, London, Paladin.

Bateson, G. (1978), Addendum 2, 'Theory versus Empiricism', in M. Berger (ed.), *Beyond the Double Bind*, New York, Brunner.

Bhaskar, R. (1978), *A Realist Theory of Science*, Brighton, Harvester.

Binswanger, L. (1963), *Being-in-the-World*, translated by J. Needlemaun, New York, Basic Books.

Blaxter, M. (1981), *The Health of the Children: A Review of Research on the Place of Health in Cycles of Disadvantage*, London, Heinemann.

Bloch, S. and Chodoff, P. (1981) (eds), *Psychiatric Ethics*, Oxford, Oxford University Press.

Boszormenyi-Nagy, I. (1965), 'Intensive family therapy as process', in I. Boszormenyi-Nagy and J. Framo (eds), *Intensive Family Therapy*, New York, Harper & Row.

Boszormenyi-Nagy, I. and Spark, G. (1973), *Invisible Loyalties*, New York, Harper & Row.

Bowen, M. (1972), 'Toward the differentiation of a self in one's own family', in J. Framo (ed.), *Family Interaction*, Springer, New York.

Bowen, M. (1978), *Family Therapy in Clinical Practice*, New York, Jason Aronson.

Bowlby, J. (1951), *Maternal Care and Mental Health*, Geneva, World Health Organisation.

Bowlby, J. (1953), *Child Care and the Growth of Love*, London, Pelican, 2nd edn, 1965.

Bowlby, J. (1969), *Attachment and Loss*, vol, 1, London, Hogarth Press.

Bowlby, J. (1980), *Attachment and Loss*, vol. 3, London, Hogarth Press.

Breunlin, D.C., Cornwell, M. and Cade, B.W. (1983), 'International trade in family therapy; parallels between societal and therapeutic values,' in C.J. Falicov (ed.), *Cultural Perspectives in Family Therapy*, Maryland, Aspen Systems Corporation.

British Association of Social Workers (1975), *A Code of Ethics for Social Work*, Birmingham, BASW.

British Medical Association (1984), *The Handbook of Medical Ethics*, London, BMA.

British Psychological Society (1978), *Ethical Principles for Research with Human Subjects*, Leicester, BPS.

British Psychological Society (1983), *Guidelines for the Professional Practice of Clinical Psychology*, Leicester, BPS.

British Psychological Society (1985), 'A Code of Conduct for Psychologists', *Bulletin of the British Psychological Society*, 38.

Brodsky, A.M. (1980), 'A decade of feminist influence on psychotherapy', *Psychology of Women Quarterly*, 4.

Broverman, I.K. *et al.* (1970), 'Sex-role stereotypes and clinical judgements of mental health', *Journal of Consulting and Clinical Psychology*, 34.

Buber, M. (1923), *Ich und Du*, translated by R.C. Smith, *I and Thou*, 2nd edition, New York, Charles Scribners & Sons, 1958.

Bucher, R. and Stelling, J.G. (1977), *Becoming Professional*, New York, Sage.

Byng-Hall, J. (1973), 'Family Myths used as Defence in Conjoint-Family Therapy', *Brit. J. of Med. Psychology*, 46.

Byng-Hall, J. (1980), 'Symptom bearer as marital distance regulator: clinical implications', *Family Process*, 19.

Cade, B. (1979), 'The use of paradox in therapy', in Walrond-Skinner (1979).

Cade, B.W. (1984), 'Unpredictability and change; a holographic metaphor' in G. Weeks (ed.), *Promoting Change Through Paradoxical Therapy*, Homeward, Illinois, Dow Jones-Irwin.

Cade, B. and Seligman, P. (1981), *Association for Child Psychology and Psychiatry Newsletter*, 6.

Calof, D.L. (1984), 'An exchange of identities', *The Family Therapy Networker*, 8.

Campbell, A.V. (1981), 'Moral autonomy', in Duncan *et al.* (1981).

Carpenter, J. (1984), 'Child guidance and family therapy', in Treacher and Carpenter (1984).

Carter, E. and McGoldnick, M. (1980) (eds), *The Family Life Cycle – a framework for family therapy*, New York, Gardner Press.

Caust, B. *et al*, 'Challenges and promises of training women as family systems therapists', *Family Process*, 20.

Chesler, P. (1971), 'Patient and patriarch: women in the psychotherapeutic relationship', in V. Gornick and B.K. Moran (eds), *Women in Sexist Society*, New York, Basic Books.

Chesler, P. (1972), *Women and Madness*, New York, Doubleday.

Chodorow, N. (1978), *The Reproduction of Mothering*, California, University of California Press.

Clayre, A. (1984), *The Heart of the Dragon*, London, Collins/Harvill.

Collier, A.S. (1977), *R.D. Laing: the Philosophy and Politics of Psychotherapy*, Hassocks, Harvester.

Collier, A.S. (1979), 'In defence of epistemology', in Mepham and Ruben (eds) (1979).

Crowell, M.G.J. (1981), 'Feminism and modern psychoanalysis: a response to feminist critics of psychoanalysis' *Modern Psychoanalysis*, 6.

Dahlberg, C. (1970), 'Sexual contact between patient and therapist', *Contemporary Psychoanalysis*, 6.

Davidson, D. (1980), *Essays on Actions and Events*, Oxford, Oxford University Press.

Davie, R., Butler, N. and Goldstein, H. (1972), *From Birth to Seven*, London, Longman.

Dell, P. (1980), 'Researching the Family Theories of Schizophrenia: an exercise in epistemological confusion', *Family Process*, 19.

Dell, P. (1981), 'Some irreverent thoughts on paradox', *Family Process*, 20.

Dell, P. (1981), A workshop on 1–2 May at the City Centre, London.

Dell, P. (1982), 'Beyond homeostasis: Toward a concept of coherence', *Family Process*, 21.

Dennis, N., Henriques, F. and Slaughter, C. (1969), *Coal is Our Life*, London, Tavistock.

Dimmock, B. and Dungworth, D. (1983), 'Creating manoeuvrability for family/systems therapists in social services departments', *Journal of Family Therapy*, 5.

Dimmock, B. and Dungworth, D. (1985), 'Beyond the family; using network meetings with statutory child care cases', *Journal of Family Therapy*, 7.

Donnison, D. (1984), 'Social Policy: an egalitarian view', *Community Care*, 11 October.

Dowling, E. (1979), 'Co-therapy: a clinical researcher's view', in Walrond-Skinner, S. (1979).

Dowling, E. (1985), 'The struggle for control in family therapy: means to an end or an end in itself?', *Journal of Family Therapy*, 7.

Downie, R.S. (1966), 'Objective and reactive attitudes', *Analysis* 27, 2.

Downie, R.S. (1971), *Roles and Values: an introduction to social ethics*, London, Methuen.

Dryden, W. (1984) (ed.), *Individual Therapy in Britain*, London, Harper & Row.

Duncan, A.S., Dunstan, G.R. and Welbourn, R.B. (1981) (eds), *Dictionary of Medical Ethics*, London, Darton, Longman & Todd.

Dunstan, G.R. (1981), 'Medical Ethics', in Duncan *et al.* (1981).

Dunstan, G.R. (1982), *Therapy and Care: Psychodynamic and Theological Images of Man*, the Malcolm Miller Lecture (1981), Aberdeen University Press, Aberdeen.

Editorial (1981), 'Social work, sociology and the context of family therapy', *Journal of Family Therapy*, 3.

Emery, F.E. (1969), *Systems Thinking: Selected Readings*, Harmondsworth, Penguin.

Epstein, N.B. and Bishop, D.S. (1981), 'Problem-centred systems therapy of the family', in A.S. Gurman and D.P. Kniskern (eds), *Handbook of Family Therapy*, New York, Brunner-Mazel.

Erickson, E. (1976), 'Psychoanalysis and ethics – avowed and unavowed', *International Review of Psychoanalysis*, 3.

Erickson, G., Rachlis, R. and Tobin, M. (1974), 'Combined family and service network intervention', *Social Worker*, (Canada), 41.

Fagin, L. and Little, M. (1984), *The Forsaken Families*, Harmondsworth, Penguin.

Fahlberg, V. (1981), *Attachment and Separation*, London, British Agencies for Adoption and Fostering.

Feldman, L.B. and Pinsof, W. (1982), 'Problem maintenance in family systems: an integrative model', *Journal of Marital and Family Therapy*, 8.

Ferri, E. (1976), 'Growing up in a one-parent family', *Concern*, 20.

Fletcher, R. (1966), *The Family and Marriage in Britain*, Harmondsworth, Penguin.

Fisch, R. *et al.* (1983), *Tactics of Change: Doing therapy briefly*, San Francisco, Jossey Bass.

Fisch, R. (1984), 'Commentary', *The Family Therapy Networker*, 8.

Flax, J. (1978), 'The conflict between nurturance and autonomy in mother-daughter relationships and within feminism', *Feminist Studies*, 4.

Ford, J. and Hollick, M. (1979), 'The Singer or the Song? An autobiographical account of a suicidal destructive person and her social worker', in *British Journal of Social Work*, 9.

Ford, J. (1983), *Human Behaviour: Towards a practical understanding*, London, Routledge & Kegan Paul.

Foster, J.G. (1971), *Enquiry into the Practice and Effects of Scientology*, London, HMSO.

Frankl, V. (1973), *Psychotherapy and Existentialism*, Harmondsworth, Pelican.

Freud, S. (1920), 'The psychogenesis of a case of female homosexuality', *Standard Edition*, 18, London, Hogarth Press.

Freud, S. (1925), 'Some psychical consequences of the anatomical distinction between the sexes', *Standard Edition*, 19, London, Hogarth Press.

Freud, S. (1931), 'Female sexuality', *Standard Edition*, 21, London, Hogarth Press.

Freud, S. (1933), 'Femininity', *Standard Edition*, 22, London, Hogarth Press.

Garrison, J. (1974), 'Network techniques: case studies in the screening-linking-planning conference method', *Family Process*, 13.

Gilbert, W.S. (1876), *The Savoy Operas*, London, Macmillan.

Gittings, D. (1985), *The Family in Question: Changing Households and Familiar Ideologies*, London, Macmillan.

Goldberg, C. (1977), *Therapeutic Partnership: ethical concerns in psychotherapy*, New York, Springer.

Golder, V. (1985), 'Feminism and family therapy', *Family Process*, 24.

Gore, W.R. (1972), 'The relationship between sex roles, marital status and mental illness', *Social Forces*, 51.

Gore, W.R. and Tudor, J. (1973), 'Adult sex roles and mental illness', *American Journal of Sociology*, 78.

Gorrell-Barnes, G. (1984), *Working with families*, London, Macmillan.

Graham, K. (1977), *J.L. Austin, A Critique of Ordinary Language Philosophy*, Brighton, Harvester.

Graham, K. (1982), 'Democracy and the autonomous moral agent' in K. Graham (ed.), *Contemporary Political Philosophy*, Cambridge, Cambridge University Press.

Green, S.L. and Hansen, J.C. (1986) 'Ethical dilemmas in family therapy', *Journal of Marital and Family Therapy*, 12.

Guggenbuhl-Craig, A. (1982), *Power and the Helping Professions*, Spring Publications, Dallas.

Gurman, A.S. (1981), 'Integrative marital therapy', in Budman, S.H. (ed.), *Forms of Brief Therapy*, New York, Guildford Press.

Gurman, A.S. and Kniskern, D.P. (1978), 'Deterioration in marital and family therapy', *Family Process*, 17.

Haines, J. (1975), *Skills and Methods in Social Work*, London, Constable.

Haldane, D. and McCluskey, U. (1982), 'Existentialism and family therapy: a neglected perspective', *Journal of Family Therapy*, 4.

Haldane, D., McCluskey, U. and Clark, D. (1986), 'Does marriage matter: a perspective and model for action', *Journal of Social Work Practice*, 2.

Haldane, J.D., McCluskey, U. and Peacey, M. (1980), 'Development of a residential facility for families in Scotland: prospect and retrospect', *International Journal of Family Psychiatry*, 3.

Haley, J. and Hoffman, L. (1967) (eds), *Techniques of Family Therapy*, New York, Basic Books.

Haley, J. (1976a), *Problem Solving Therapy*, San Francisco, Jossey Bass.

Haley, J. (1976b), 'Development of a theory', in C.E. Sluzki and D.E. Ranson, *Double Bind: The Foundation of the Communication Approach to the Family*, New York, Grune & Stratton.

Hare-Mustin, R. (1978), 'A feminist approach to family therapy', *Family Process*, 17.

Hartman, W.E. and Fithian, M.A. (1972), *Treatment of Sexual Dysfunction*, California, Centre for Marital and Sexual Studies.

Hayes, J. and Nutman, P. (1981), *Understanding the Unemployed*, London, Tavistock.

Heard, D.H. (1978), 'From object relations to attachment theory: A basis for family therapy', *British Journal of Medical Psychology*, 51, 1.

Heard, D.H. (1981), 'The relevance of attachment theory to child psychiatric practice', *Journal of Child Psychology and Psychiatry*, 22.

Her Majesty's Stationery Office (1948), *Criminal Justice Act 1948*, sec 6(1), London.

Her Majesty's Stationery Office (1983), *Mental Health Act*, London.

Hines, P.M. and Hare-Mustin, R. (1981), 'Ethical concerns in family therapy', in Hanson, J.C. and Rosenthal, D. (eds), *Strategies and Techniques in Family Therapy*, Springfield, Ill, Charles C. Thomas.

Hoffman, L. (1971), 'Deviation-Amplifying Processes in Natural Groups', in Haley, J. (ed.), *Changing Families*, New York, Grune & Stratton.

Hollis, F. (1964), *Casework: A Psychosocial Therapy*, New York, Random House Press.

Horney, K. (1967), *Feminine Psychology*, Norton, New York.

Hudson, P. (1980), 'Different strokes for different folks', *Journal of Family Therapy*, 2.

Illich, I. (1975), *Medical Nemesis – The Expropriation of Health*, London, Calder & Boyars.

Illich, I. and McKnight, J. (1977), *Disabling Professions*, London.

Jabubowski, P. (1977), 'Assertive behaviour and clinical problems of women', in E. Rawlings, and D. Carter (eds), *Psychotherapy for Women*, Springfield, Ill., Charles C. Thomas.

Jordan, W. (1981), 'Family therapy – an outsider's view', *Journal of Family Therapy*, 3.

Jung, C.G. (1953), 'Two essays on analytical psychology', *Collected Works*, London, Routledge & Kegan Paul.

Kant, I. (1785), *Groundwork of the Metaphysic of Morals*, in H.J. Paton, editor and translator (1949), *The Moral Law*, London, Hutchinson.

Kantor, D. and Lehr, W. (1973), *Inside the Family*, San Francisco, Jossey Bass.

Karasu, T. (1981), 'Ethical aspects of psychotherapy', in Bloch and Chodoff (eds) (1981).

Kardener, S. *et al.* (1973), 'A survey of physicians' attitudes and practices regarding erotic and non-erotic contact with patients', *American Journal of Psychiatry*, 130.

Keeney, B.P. and Sprenkle, D.H. (1982), 'Ecosystemic epistemology: critical implications for the aesthetics and pragmatics of family therapy', *Family Process*, 21.

Kellmer Pringle, M. (1975), *The Needs of Children*, London, Hutchinson.

Kennedy, I. (1981), *Unmasking Medicine*, London, Allen & Unwin.

Kingston, P. (1982), 'Power and influence in the environment of family therapy', *Journal of Family Therapy*, 4.

Klein, M. (1952), 'Some theoretical conclusions regarding the emotional life of the infant', in *Writings of Melanie Klein*, vol 3, London, Hogarth Press.

Kraemer, S. (1981), 'Why the question is missing: a reply to Kerreen Reiger's paper', *Journal of Family Therapy*, 3.

Kraemer, S. (1983), 'Why I am not a family therapist', *Changes*, 2.

Kubler-Ross, E. (1975), *Death: the final stage of growth*, Englewood Cliffs, New Jersey, Prentice-Hall.

Laing, R.D. and Esterson, A. (1970), *Sanity, Madness and the Family*, Harmondsworth, Penguin.

Levant, R. (1978), 'Family therapy: a client centred perspective', *Journal of Marriage and Family Counselling*, 4.

Lewis, J.M. *et al.* (1976), *No Single Thread: Psychological Health in Family Systems*, New York, Brunner Mazel.

Libow, J.A. *et al.*, (1982), 'Feminist and family systems therapy: are they irreconcilable', *American Journal of Family Therapy*, 10.

Liddle, H. (1982), 'On the problem of eclecticism: a call for epistemologic clarification and human scale theories; *Family Process*, 21.

Lieberman, S. (1979), *Transgenerational Family Therapy*, London, Croom Helm.

Lindley, R. (1986), *Autonomy*, London, Macmillan.

Lipman-Blumen, J. (1975), 'A crisis framework applied to micro-sociological family changes: marriage, divorce and occupational trends associated with World War II, *Journal of Marriage and the Family*, 37.

Lorion, R.P. (1978), 'Research on psychotherapy and behaviour change with the disadvantaged', in S.L. Garfield and A.E. Bergin (eds), *Handbook of Psychotherapy and Behaviour Change*, New York, Wiley.

McGoldrick, M., Pearce, J.K. and Giordano, J. (1982), *Ethnicity and Family Therapy*, New York, Guildford Press.

MacMurray, J. (1932), *Freedom in the Modern World*, London, Faber & Faber.

MacMurray, J. (1957), *The Self as Agent*, London, Faber & Faber.

MacMurray, J. (1961), *Persons in Relation*, London, Faber & Faber.

Marris, P. (1974), *Loss and Change*, London, Routledge & Kegan Paul.

Maruyama, M. (1968), 'The Second Cybernetics', in W. Buckley (ed.), *Modern Systems Research for the Behavioural Scientist*, Chicago, Aldine.

Marx, K. (1845), *The German Ideology* (various editions).

Masters, W. and Johnson, V.E. (1970), *Human Sexual Inadequacy*, Boston, Little Brown.

Masters, W. *et al.* (1977), *Ethical Issues in Sex Therapy and Research*, Boston, Little Brown.

Mattinson, J. and Sinclair, I. (1979), *Mate and Stalemate*, Oxford, Blackwell.

Mepham, J. and Ruben, D.H. (1979) (eds), *Issues in Marxist Philosophy*, vol. 3, Brighton, Harvester.

Meyer, A. (1957), *Psychobiology: a science of man*, Springfield, Illinois, Charles C. Thomas.

Mill, J.S. (1843), *A System of Logic*, London, Longmans, Green.

Miller, J.B. (1976), *Toward a New Psychology of Women*, Harmondsworth, Penguin.

Minuchin, S. (1974), *Families and Family Therapy*, London, Tavistock.

Minuchin, S. and Fishman, H.C. (1981), *Family Therapy Techniques*, London, Harvard.

Mitchell, J. (1974), *Psychoanalysis and Feminism*, Harmondsworth, Penguin.

Moberley, E. (1983), *Psychogenesis*, London, Routledge & Kegan Paul.

Morgan, D. (1985), *The Family, Politics and Social Theory*, London, Routledge & Kegan Paul.

Mullen, E. and Dumpson, J. (1972), 'Concluding note', in E. Mullen and J. Dumpson and Associates, *Evaluation of Social Intervention*, San Francisco, Jossey Bass.

Nagel, T. (1979), 'Death', in *Mortal Questions*, Cambridge, Cambridge University Press.

Napier, A.Y. with Whitaker, C.A. *The Family Crucible*, New York, Harper & Row.

Newsletter of the Association for Family Therapy
(1979) Whiffen, R. 'Letter from the chairman of A.F.T. to the chairman of the Joint Working Party on the Statutory Registration of Psychotherapists', May.
(1980) Gorell-Barnes, G. 'Training for family therapy. Guidelines from the sub-committee on training'. Autumn
(1983) Haldane, D. 'Report of the sub-committee on ethics'. August.
(1985) Child, N. 'A rose by any other name', March.
(1985) Hills, J. 'The argument in favour of a profession of family therapists', June.
(1985) Jenkins, H. 'A.F.T.: the development of family therapy and family therapist posts', June.
(1985) Moulin, L. 'Why I think there should not be a profession of family therapists', June.
(1985) Kingston, P. Correspondence, August.
(1985) O'Reilly, P. 'Report of the sub-committee on course approval', August.
(1985) Wilkins, R. 'Report of the sub-committee on ethics', August.
(1985) Child, N. 'An open letter to the chairman', December.
(1985) Aspin, J. 'A plea for sound mind', December.

Nursten, J., Pettinger, J. and Anderson, M. (1972), *Social Workers and Their Clients*, London, Research Publication Services.

Olson, D.H. *et al.* (1983), 'Marital and family therapy: a decade review', in D.H. Olson and B.C. Miller (eds), *Family Studies Yearbook*, Beverly Hills, Sage.

Osborne, K. (1983), 'Women in families: feminist therapy and family systems', *Journal of Family Therapy*, 5.

Palazzoli, M.S. (1981), 'Comments on Paul Dell's "Some irreverent thoughts on Paradox"', *Family Process*, 20.

Palazzoli, M.S. (1983), 'The emergence of a comprehensive systems approach',

Journal of Family Therapy, 5.

Palazzoli, M.S. (1984), 'Behind the scenes of the organisation: some guidelines for the expert in human relations', *Journal of Family Therapy*, 6.

Palazzoli, M.S. (1985), 'The emergence of a comprehensive systems approach: Supervisor and team problems in a district psychiatric centre, *Journal of Family Therapy*, 7.

Palazzoli, M.S., Boscolo, E., Cecchin, G. and Prata, G. (1978), *Paradox and Counter Paradox*, New York, Jason Aronson.

Papp, P. (1983), *The Process of Change*, New York, Guildford Press.

Parkes, G.M. (1972), *Bereavement: studies of grief in adult life*, New York, International Universities Press.

Parkes, C.M. and Stevenson-Hinde, J. (1982) (eds), *The Place of Attachment in Human Behaviour*, London, Tavistock.

Peterfreund, E. (1971), 'Information, systems and psychoanalysis', *Psychological Issues*, 7, 1–2.

Piercy, F.P. *et al.* (1983), 'Ethical, legal and professional issues in family therapy: a graduate level course', *Journal of Marital and Family Therapy*, 9.

Pilalis, J. (1984), 'The formalisation of family therapy training, issues and implications', *Journal of Family Therapy*, 4.

Pincus, L. (1974), *Death and the Family*, London, Faber & Faber.

Pincus, A. and Minahan, A. (1973), *Social Work Practice: Model and Method*, Itasca, Illinois, E.E. Peacock.

Radcliffe-Richards, J. (1980), *The Sceptical Feminist*, London, Routledge & Kegan Paul.

Reiger, K. (1981), 'Family therapy's missing question, why the plight of the modern family?', *Journal of Family Therapy*, 3.

Richter, H.E. (1974), *The Family as Patient: the origin, nature and treatment of marital and family conflicts*, London, Souvenir.

Rochford, G. (1981), 'Love, care, control and punishment', *Journal of Family Therapy*, 3.

Roddoff, L. (1975), 'Sex differences in depression: the effects of occupation and marital status', *Sex Roles*, 1.

Rogers, C. (1961), *On Becoming a Person: a therapist's view of psychotherapy*, Boston, Houghton Mifflin.

Rogers, C. (1969), *Encounter Groups*, Harmondsworth, Penguin.

Roman, M. *et al.* (1978), 'The value system of psychotherapists and changing moves', *Psychotherapy: theory, research and practice*, 15.

Rousseau, J-J. (1966), *The Social Contract*, London, Dent.

Russell, B. (1917), 'On the notion of cause', in *Mysticism and Logic*, London, George Allen & Unwin.

Satir, V. (1967), *Conjoint Family Therapy: a guide to theory and technique*, Palo Alto, Science and Behaviour Books.

Satir, V. (1976), *Peoplemaking*, Palo Alto, Science and Behaviour Books.

Sayers, J. (1982), *Biological Politics: feminist and antifeminist perspectives*, London, Tavistock.

Scheflen, A.E. (1981), *Levels of Schizophrenia*, New York, Brunner Mazel.

Schmideberg, M. (1978), 'Penetrating analysis – an interview with Dr M. Schmideberg by Phil Mollon', *New Forum, The Journal of the Psychology and Psychotherapy Association*, 5.

Shotter, E. (1981), 'The Journal of Medical Ethics', in Duncan *et al.* 1981.

Sieghart, P. (1978), *Statutory Registration of Psychotherapists: A Report of a Professions Joint Working Party*, Cambridge, E.E. Plumridge.

Singer, P. (1980), *Practical Ethics*, Cambridge, Cambridge University Press.

Skynner, A.C.R. (1976), *One Flesh, Separate Persons*, London, Constable.

Skynner, A.C.R. and Cleese, J. (1983), *Families and How to Survive Them*, London, Methuen.

Slipp, S., Ellis, S. and Kreasel, K. (1974), 'Factors associated with engagement in family therapy', *Family Process*, 13.

Sonne, J. and Lincoln, G. (1965), 'Heterosexual co-therapy relationships and their significance in family therapy' in *Psychology for the Whole Family*, New York, Springer.

Speck, R. and Attneave, C. (1973), *Family Networks*, New York, Pantheon.

Speck, R. and Rueveni, U. (1969), 'Network therapy – a developing concept, *Family Process*, 8.

Spiegel, R. (1978), 'On psychoanalysis, values and ethics', *Journal of American Academy of Psychoanalysis*, 6.

Stanton, M.D. (1980), 'Marital therapy from a structural/strategic viewpoint', in G.P. Sholevar (ed.), *Handbook of Marriage and Marital Therapy*, Lancaster, MTP Press.

Stanton, D. (1981), 'The strategic approaches', in Gurman, A.S. and Kniskern, D.P. (eds), *Handbook of Family Therapy*, New York, Brunner Mazel.

Stock, W. *et al.* (1982), 'Women and psychotherapy, *International Journal of Mental Health*, 11.

Store, A.A. (1976), 'The legal implications of sexual activity between psychiatrist and patient', *American Journal of Psychiatry*, 133.

Strawson, P.F. (1959), *Individuals*, London, Methuen.

Strawson, P.F. (1968), 'Freedom and resentment' in Strawson, P.F. (ed.), *Studies in the Philosophy of Thought and Action*, Oxford, Oxford University Press.

Treacher, A. (1986), 'Invisible patients, invisible families – an exploration of some technocratic trends in family therapy', *Journal of Family Therapy*, 8.

Treacher, A. and Carpenter, J. (1984) (eds), *Using Family Therapy*, Oxford, Blackwell.

Tsoi-Hoshmund, L. (1976), 'Marital therapy and changing values', *Family Co-ordinator*, 25.

Tunstall, J. (1962), *The Fisherman*, London, McGibbon & Kee.

Tuson, G. (1985), 'Philosophy and family therapy. A study in interconnectedness', *Journal of Family Therapy*, 7.

Walrond-Skinner, S. (1976), *Family Therapy*, London, Routledge & Kegan Paul.

Walrond-Skinner, S. (1979), (ed.), *Family and Marital Psychotherapy: a Critical Approach*, London, Routledge & Kegan Paul.

Walrond-Skinner, S. (1981) (ed.), *Developments in Family Therapy*, London, Routledge & Kegan Paul.

Walters, M. *et al.* (1981), 'The dilemma of women in families: implications for family therapy', *Women's Project in Family Therapy*, 1st International Conference, London.

Watson, D. (1985) (ed.), *A Code of Ethics for Social Work: the Second Step*, London, Routledge & Kegan Paul.

Watzlawick, P., Beavin, J. and Jackson, D.D. (1967), *Pragmatics of Human Communication*, New York, Norton.

Watzlawick, P., Weakland, J. and Fisch, R. (1974), *Change: Principles of Problem*

Formation and Problem Resolution, New York, Norton.

Weakland, J., Fisch, R., Watzlawick, P. and Bodin, A.M. (1974), 'Brief Therapy: focussed problem resolution', *Family Process*, 13.

Wedge, P. and Prosser, H. (1973), *Born to Fail?* London, Arrow Books.

Wender, P. (1971), 'Vicious and virtuous circles', in Barten, H. (ed.), *Brief Therapies*, New York, Behavioural Publications.

Whitaker, C. (1975), 'The growing edge', in J. Haley and L. Hoffman (eds), *Techniques of Family Therapy*, New York, Basic Books.

Whitaker, C.A. (1982), *From Psyche to System: the evolving therapy of Carl Whitaker*, New York, Guildford Press.

Winnicott, D.W. (1941), 'The Observation of Infants in a Set Situation', in *Collected Papers: through paediatrics to psychoanalysis*, London, Tavistock, 1958.

Winnicott, D.W. (1957), 'The ordinary devoted mother and her baby', in *The Child and the Family*, Part I, London, Tavistock.

Winnicott, D.W. (1960), 'Ego distortion in terms of true and false self', in *The Maturational Process and the Facilitating Environment*, London, Hogarth Press, 1965.

Woodfield, A. (1976), *Teleology*, Cambridge, Cambridge University Press.

Wootton, B. (1959), *Social Science and Social Pathology*, London, Allen & Unwin.

INDEX